CHRISTIAN DISCIPLESHIP

IN THE
TWENTY-FIRST CENTURY

To Inez,
Thank you for your
encouragement and support.
May God continue to
richly bless you and keep
you.
Rev. Zacky R. Johnson

Dr. Zackary R. Johnson, Sr.

Published by

Hadassah's Crown Publishing, LLC

634 NE Main St #1263

Simpsonville, SC 29681

Paperback Edition ISBN: 978-1-960779-13-7

Printed in the United States

To my wife, Sandra, for her love, support and encouragement to me in every area of life. In addition, I dedicate this book to our children: Charles, Bridgette and Zackary, Jr. for their love and support.

FOREWORD

In the Fall of 2020 during the most intense season of the pandemic, I had the privilege of meeting Zackary Johnson, a seasoned pastor who was working on his Doctor of Ministry degree at Erskine Theological Seminary, where I earned my degrees and served as an adjunct professor. My assigned task was to work with, and advise, Zackary in the development, research, and writing of his book, which became the basis for this book. Quickly, I learned to respect Zackary not just for his solid work, but for his passionate commitment to Christ and His church.

In the process of working with Zack, he became a trusted friend and colleague. In our conversations and work together, I began to realize that his book was not just an academic exercise. What I was reading in Zackary's book I was also seeing in his life and ministry. As he developed the biblical basis for his work, tracing discipleship throughout the book of Acts, I observed the ways he was putting those biblical concepts into practice.

Many pastors in Zackary's season of life would choose to coast through the latter years of ministry into retirement, but not Zackary. Long past the time when most people would be "hanging it up," so to speak, Zackary was researching and learning about the characteristics of Generations X, Y, and Z, seeking to help the church be more effective in reaching these generations of disciples who have less loyalty to denominational affiliations and are less likely to think of the church in institutional terms.

What you will find in this book is an honest look at what it will take for the church to reach new generations with the transforming power of the gospel of Jesus Christ: authenticity, a relational approach to ministry, transparency, humility and integrity, as well as sound biblical teaching and preaching. For Zackary, these are not just lofty, academic ideals, but actual touchstones of Zackary's own life and ministry. If there were ever an author who follows his own advice, fleshes out what he writes, and practices what he preaches, it is Zackary. And because of his own personal commitment to Christ and the church, Zackary's words in this book will come alive in the life of the reader just as they have in the life of the author.

— Stephen Clyborne

Senior Pastor, Earle Street Baptist Church, Greenville, SC

Jesus wanted everyone to know that the kingdom of God is available to all who seek Him as Lord and Savior.

— Dr. Zackary Johnson, Sr.

CONTENTS

...it is evident that many people understand more about the institution of the church than they do about the individual call to discipleship.

— Dr. Zackary Johnson, Sr.

INTRODUCTION

This is a scholarly resource designed to aid members of the church in moving from membership to discipleship by being committed followers and students of Jesus Christ through learning, teaching, emulating and dedication. The overall objective is to provide information that will help Christians understand the importance of becoming a disciple for Jesus Christ through the following:

1. understanding the meaning of a disciple and discipleship
2. discovering the impact of the Kingdom of God on discipleship
3. surveying discipleship in the book of Acts
4. exploring discipleship in the twenty-first century.

A problem in many churches today is that they are driven more by tradition than mission, driven by these seven last words:

"We've never done it this way before." Change is almost impossible in this type of traditional church that looks down on strangers who walk in the church, is more concerned with taking care of those who are within the church rather than those who are outside the church, and is focused more on the Constitution/Bylaws than the spiritual growth of the people. In this kind of church, there is more of a country club mentality than a spirit of inclusiveness of all people.

The root of the problem is that many churches have more members than disciples. There are members who have attended church for most of their lives, but don't understand discipleship. Therefore, many churches are dying because the members don't understand what it means to be a disciple and their role in the discipleship process. They don't clearly understand the great commission that Jesus gave us: "Go therefore and make disciples of all the nations, baptizing them in the name of the Father and of the Son and of the Holy Spirit, teaching them to observe all things that I have commanded you; and lo, I am with you always, even to the end of the age. Amen" (Matthew 28:19-20).

There is a need for church members to understand for themselves what it means to be a disciple so that they may be effective in making disciples.

There is a need for church members to understand for themselves what it means to be a disciple so that they may be effective in making disciples. How can people make disciples if they are not disciples themselves? There is a need for members to be spiritually mature, and for churches to transform members into disciples if they are going to experience numerical growth in the twenty-first century.

There is a Biblical basis for the church moving from a traditional mindset to a missional mindset that begins as early as Genesis 1:1: "In the beginning God created the heavens and the earth." God did not create heaven and earth for Himself. God created heaven and earth for humankind. Then God made humans in His image and likeness, and gave them dominion over all the earth. In essence, they were given authority over every living thing on the face of the earth. God did not want the man to live alone so he a created a woman from the man to be his helper. So, God gave Adam the authority to name all of the creatures including woman who was taken out of the man. In addition, God gave Adam some instructions for the Garden of Eden: "Of every tree of the garden you may freely eat; but of the tree of the knowledge of good and evil you shall not eat, for in the day that you eat of it you shall surely die" (Genesis 2:16). Genesis 1-2 is very important to this book because it gives a clear picture of the sovereign power and authority of God. God had the power to create us and He can recreate us through a relationship with His Son, Jesus Christ.

In Genesis 3, the temptation fell on Adam and Eve. The serpent tempted Eve to eat of the tree and she did. Adam also ate of the tree and they both sinned against God. This sin brought eternal judgment on Adam and Eve and generations to come. After God gave them instructions on what their lives would be like going forward, He put them both out of the Garden of Eden or Paradise forever. This chapter is also very important to this book because in order for us to return back to Eden it must be by way of Jesus Christ. We must be born again disciples of Jesus Christ if we are going to return back to Eden. In Genesis 4, God gave Adam and Eve children (Cain and Abel), and Seth came along in chapter five.

Genesis 12 is probably one of the most pivotal chapters in the Old Testament. In this chapter, the Lord told Abram to leave his country, his people and his father's household to go to a strange land that He would show Him. Imagine Abraham having enough faith in God to go to a strange land that he knew nothing about. God made three promises to Abram: you will be a great nation, your name will be blessed, and you and many generations will be blessed through you. So at seventy-five years old, Abram did as the Lord commanded. He took his wife Sarai, his nephew Lot, and all the possessions that they and the people had acquired in Haran, and headed out for the land of Canaan. This passage is important to this book because Jesus was born in the lineage of David which fulfilled the promise that God made to Abram. Also, this chapter shows God's concern not just for Abram and his descendants, but also for all the families of the earth.

Even though it should have taken the children of Israel only a short time to get to the land of Canaan, it took them over forty years. Through the lineage of Abraham, Isaac and Jacob, many terrible things faced the children of Israel including captivity in Babylon. During this time God sent major and minor prophets to give the Israelites instructions. At times the covenant people obeyed, but many times they failed to obey. In addition, God also sent prophets to prophesy about the coming Messiah, who would come to save His people and all the world from their sins. The prophet Isaiah wrote, "For to us a child is born, to us a son is given, and the government will be on his shoulders. And he will be called Wonderful Counselor, Mighty God, Everlasting Father, Prince of Peace" (Isaiah 9:6). In Isaiah 53:5-6, the prophet made God's redemptive plan so clear: "But He *was* wounded for our transgressions, *He was* bruised for our iniquities; The chastisement for our peace *was* upon Him, And by His stripes we are healed. All we like sheep have gone astray; We have turned, every one, to his own way; And the LORD has laid on Him the iniquity of us all." The passages in Isaiah are important to this book because the Old Testament clearly prophesied about the coming Messiah and what He would bring to all mankind.

Before the coming of the Messiah in the New Testament there were 400 years of silence, also called **the intertestamental period.** The 400 years of silence refers to the time when God did not speak to the Jewish people. That period of time began with the warning that closed the Old Testament in Malachi 4:5-6: "Behold, I am going to send you Elijah the prophet before the coming of the great and terrible day of the LORD. He will restore the hearts of the fathers to their children and the hearts of the children to their fathers, so that I will not come and smite the land with a curse." This passage of scripture is important to this book because it prepares God's people for the coming Messiah introduced by John the Baptist, the Messiah's forerunner and the importance of receiving Him before the end times.

In the New Testament, there is a clear picture of the divinity and incarnation of Jesus Christ. In John 1:1, we find these words: "In the beginning was the Word, and the Word was with God, and the Word was God." The opening line parallels the opening line of Genesis 1:1, which begins with the same words: "In the beginning..." The Word (*logos*) was with God from the beginning. The word *logos* means the Word of God, or principle of divine reason and creative order. It is identified in the Gospel of John with the second person of the Trinity, incarnate in Jesus Christ. The prologue of John's Gospel (1:1-18) begins and ends in eternity, which effectively emphasizes the Word entering time and history through the incarnation (1:14). The prologue clearly asserts the divinity of Jesus Christ. Themes introduced in the prologue such as light, life, darkness, witness, faith, glory, and truth are more fully developed throughout the Gospel of John. The prologue was built on loaded words like *word* (1:1), *light* and *life* (1:4-5), *world* (1:9-10), *believe* (1:7), and *flesh* (1:14). The prologue of John's Gospel is important to the book because Jesus was very much God and man at the same time. The principle of the incarnation introduced in the prologue became the guiding theme for John's entire Gospel, so that we must distinguish throughout the life of Jesus of Nazareth His human nature and the mystery of "the Son who comes from the Father," a mystery that reveals itself in Christ Jesus the man.

According to Luke, Jesus quoted from Isaiah's prophecy in His first sermon in Nazareth: "The Spirit of the LORD *is* upon Me, Because He has anointed Me To preach the gospel to *the* poor; He has sent Me to heal the brokenhearted, To proclaim liberty to *the* captives and recovery of sight to *the* blind, to set at liberty those who are oppressed" (Luke 4:18). Jesus brought redemption to all humankind to set people free from sin and evil. The redemption would be to Jews and Gentiles alike which was prophesied in Isaiah 49:6: "Indeed He says, 'It is too small a thing that You should be My Servant To raise up the tribes of Jacob, And to restore the preserved ones of Israel; I will also give You as a light to the Gentiles, That You should be My salvation to the ends of the earth.'" He eventually was crucified, dead and buried, but arose on the third day with power and authority in His hands. In Luke 24:7, He said, "The Son of Man must be delivered into the hands of sinful men, and be crucified, and the third day rise again."

And finally, Jesus gave us the great commission before His ascension: "All authority has been given to Me in heaven and on earth. Go therefore and make disciples of all the nations, baptizing them in the name of the Father and of the Son and of the Holy Spirit, teaching them to observe all things that I have commanded you; and lo, I am with you always, *even* to the end of the age. Amen" (Matthew 28:19-20). The great commission is important to this book because it is the believer's marching orders to do the mission work that needs to be done. Redemption involves missions. So based on the great commission we are to make disciples who go out and make other disciples. Discipleship takes place when we bring all of life under the Lordship of Jesus Christ. The driving force behind this process is the Holy Spirit who will lead and guide us in doing the mission work that Christ has commissioned us to do.

A good example of the Holy Spirit's power is on the Day of Pentecost when the church was founded. In the book of

Acts we see how salvation was brought to all people. In Acts chapter two, Peter preached an awesome salvation message about the power of Jesus Christ. When the people heard it, they were cut to the heart and said to Peter and the rest of the disciples in verses 37 and 38, "Men *and* brethren, what shall we do?" Then Peter said unto them, "Repent, and be baptized every one of you in the name of Jesus Christ for the remission of sins, and ye shall receive the gift of the Holy Ghost." Therefore, the church is not about us. It is about the life-changing gospel of Jesus Christ. The church must be intentionally focused in every part of its life on the mission of God in the world. The main Biblical basis for this book is the great commission calling for the church to transform members into Spirit-filled disciples for the Kingdom of God.

This book is important because the traditional church as we know it in America is in trouble. In Mark 9, Jesus took Peter, James and John and led them up on a high mountain and was transfigured before them. Elijah with Moses appeared before them and were talking with Jesus. It must have been a Spirit-filled time because Peter wanted to stay and have three tabernacles built: one for Jesus, one for Moses and one for Elijah. As the story unfolded, Jesus did not stay. In fact, as they came down from the mountain Jesus informed them not to tell anyone until the Son of Man had risen from the dead. As He was coming down from the mountain, He came to the rest of the disciples and saw a great multitude around them, and scribes disputing with them. Jesus then asked what was being discussed. Someone in the crowd said, "Teacher, I brought You my son, who has a mute spirit. And wherever it seizes him, it throws him down; he foams at the mouth, gnashes his teeth, and becomes rigid. So I spoke to Your disciples, that they should cast it out, but they could not" (Mark 9:17-18). So as the story goes, Jesus healed the man's son, and the demon spirit came out of him. Then the disciples asked Jesus privately why they could not cast it out. Jesus said, "This kind can come out by nothing but prayer and fasting" (Mark 9:29).

In Timothy Keller's lecture, he quoted David Martyn Lloyd-Jones, who was a Welsh Protestant minister and medical doctor influential in the Reformed wing of the British evangelical movement in the twentieth century. Lloyd-Jones said, "What Jesus was also saying is that the demons are in too deep for your ordinary way of operation, your ordinary way of doing things. Your business as usual, the way you ordinarily operate, won't work with this kind."[1] The demons are in too deep for us to continue to operate the way we have been operating. In relation to the church, there is a major crisis going on right now. How do we get people back into our traditional churches in the twenty-first century, especially the Generation X (born

---

[1] Timothy Keller, *"The Supremacy of Christ in a Postmodern World: Session 3, Desiring God,"* 2009. Internet available at: https://www.youtube.com/watch?v=jMLp2mYN_D8

between 1964 and 1979), the Millennials (born between 1980 and 1994), and Generation Z (born between 1995 and 2010)? The very future of our churches will depend on reaching them over the next five to ten years. Young people seem to have more of a problem with the traditional way we do things than with God. So it is crucial that we get the gospel of Jesus Christ out in the twenty-first century because the whole notion of what is spiritual is gone. The whole notion of what is right or wrong is gone. At one time the United States was the main country carrying the gospel to the various mission fields, and now America is a mission field. And we are an anti-Christian mission field. The problem facing us is altogether deeper and more desperate than what faced the Christian church many years ago. The demons are, in fact, in too deep. Back in the day, the church was the only show in town. Church, home and school formed a community consortium that worked together to instill Christian values. People grew up as Christians simply because of the values the communities instilled. Many people were raised in a Christian home. Most church pews were full. People were aroused or excited by good singing and preaching. Church members would attend rain or shine. A couple of good singing programs and revival campaigns were enough to keep the church alive. People seemed to have more respect and reverence for God than they do now.

Many people were raised in a Christian environment, but for the most part they didn't understand or practice evangelism, mission work or discipleship. They didn't understand what it really meant to be a disciple of Jesus Christ. Churches produced a lot of members, but not many disciples. They didn't understand that they needed to have a personal relationship with Jesus Christ through the power of the Holy Spirit. For the most part they were religious but did not have a personal relationship with God through faith in Jesus. So many churches are facing a dilemma because the traditional way of getting people into churches will not work anymore. Back in the day when Mommy and Daddy said, "We're going to church," everyone went to church. Evangelistic tools with a one, two, or three-step program are no longer enough to cause people to run to church, or down the aisle. Ordinary traditional worship or evangelism outreach tools will not work anymore, because everyone seems to have some form of spirituality, even if it is the wrong spirit.

This book is important because the church needs to get back to the main mission of the great commission, and that is making disciples of Jesus Christ.

This book is important because the church needs to get back to the main mission of the great commission, and that is making disciples of Jesus Christ.

It is crucial at this point in history because many traditional churches in America have closed their doors for lack of members, and many pastors are leaving the pulpit at an alarming rate. Many churches are struggling to hold on financially on a shoestring budget. Therefore, it is important that the church in this twenty-first century transform its members into disciples. The church is not primarily about the members, but about Jesus Christ. It is important for the church to get back to the redemptive plan of God of bringing lost souls out of darkness into the marvelous light. It is high time for the church to continue to reach out to the lost rather than just maintain a place for those who are saved. The church is not a country club, but a place for transformation to take place in the lives of the people. It is high time for all members within the church to understand that they have been called not just to be members, but to be disciples. The days of hypocrisy within the church need to come to an end. The church of today needs to be more loving, caring and transparent. People don't have to air out all their dirty laundry to let people know that by the grace of God they are here; and if God can transform their lives, He can certainly transform someone else's life. The world is looking for something that is real in the midst of these turbulent times. In the midst of all the storms of life believers have the blessed hope in Christ Jesus. They are the light of the world and the salt of the earth.

Therefore, the title of the book is *Christian Discipleship in the Twenty-First Century*. The purpose of this book is to help members of the church move from membership to discipleship by being committed followers and students of Jesus Christ through learning, teaching, emulating, and dedication. The overall objective of the book is to provide information that will help Christians understand the importance of becoming a disciple for Jesus Christ. The goals of this book are first, to understand the meaning of a disciple and discipleship; second, to discover the impact of the Kingdom of God on discipleship; third, to survey discipleship in the book of Acts; fourth, to explore discipleship in the twenty-first century. There will be four major chapters in the book.

Chapter two will offer a definition of a disciple and a description of the discipleship process. Using Jesus' own teachings as a biblical foundation, this chapter will explore the lifelong process of being transformed into the image or likeness of Jesus, as well as the demands and priority of discipleship. Classic sources like Dietrich Bonhoeffer's *The Cost of Discipleship* will inform the discussion in this chapter.[2]

---

[2] Dietrich Bonhoeffer, *The Cost of Discipleship* (New York: Macmillan Publishing Co., 1979).

Chapter three will show how an understanding the Kingdom of God is essential to Christian discipleship. Again, Jesus' own teachings as well as the writings of Paul will serve as the biblical basis of the discussion, interpreted by Myles Munroe's book, *Rediscovering the Kingdom*[3], Tony Evans' book, *What a Way to Live*[4], and other sources. This chapter will help Christians understand that God has transferred them into a new domain, the domain of the Kingdom of God. The first obligation of believers is not to this world system that leaves God out, but to the Kingdom of God. In other words, a disciple is committed to the Kingdom.

Chapter four will survey discipleship in the book of Acts, and will show how the process of discipleship that Jesus used with the first disciples will transform a church and a culture. Many church growth principles are found in the book of Acts. One of the key sources for this book is John R. W. Stott's book *The Message of Acts: The Bible Speaks Today*[5], which describes the early days of the church as recorded by Luke in the book of Acts and what those early experiences have to say about issues that concern Christians today.

Chapter five will explore discipleship in the twenty-first century, and discuss the reasons why churches are declining. Why is the church losing its influence? Why is the church

---

[3] Myles Munroe, *Rediscovering The Kingdom* (Shippensburg: Destiny Image Publishers, Inc., 2004).
[4] Tony Evans, *What A Way To Live* (Nashville: Word Publishing, 1997).
[5] John R. W. Stott, *The Message of Acts: The Bible Speaks Today* (Downers Grove: InterVarsity Press, 1990).

losing its youth and young adults? Why is the church not grow-ing numerically and even spiritually? This chapter will glean insights from Thom S. Rainer and Eric Geiger's book *Simple Church: Returning to God's Process for Making Disciples*[6], *which makes the point that churches* with a clear disciple-mak-ing process are vibrant and growing. Other sources will be used to interpret changing cultural trends like Richard Niebuhr's classic work, *Christ and Culture*[7], and D. A. Carson's *Christ and Culture Revisited*[8]. Insights from Jean Twenge's book *Genera-tion Me*[9], will also inform the discussion as the characteristics of modern generations are explored. This chapter will con-clude with a description of some of the various types of disci-pleship that are effective for twenty-first century churches.

The final chapter will set forth concrete, specific, practical applications of the lessons gleaned from this book regarding Christian discipleship in the church for the twenty-first century

---

[6] Thom S. Rainer and Eric Geiger, *Simple Church: Returning to God's Process for Making Disciples* (Nashville: Broadman & Holman, 2006).
[7] Richard H. Niebuhr, *Christ and Culture* (New York, Harper, 1951).
[8] Carson, D. A., *Christ and Culture Revisited* (Grand Rapids: William B. Eerdmans Publishing, 2008).
[9] Jean M. Twenge, *Generation Me* (New York: Atria, 2014).

"*The great tragedy today is that there are not enough Christians who know who they are.*"

— **Dr. Zackary Johnson, Sr.**

CHAPTER ONE

THE MEANING OF DISCIPLE AND DISCIPLESHIP

Ask people to say who they are without giving their name, occupation, or title. How they answer that question says a lot about them. In the Bible, when people came to Jesus Christ and were dead serious about following Him, when they became people of the kingdom, from that point on there was no question about who they were. These early disciples became known even among unbelievers as people of "the Way" (Acts 19:9), because they had chosen to walk a different path in life. They had identified themselves totally with Jesus Christ and the kingdom of God. They lived for the kingdom of God and their identity was tied to the kingdom.

The great tragedy today is that there are not enough Christians who know who they are. They may be genuine believers, but their faith is just another addition to their biography. They may believe that God's Word is absolute truth and that absolute moral truth exists. They may believe that Jesus Christ lived a sinless life. They may believe that God is the all-powerful and all-knowing Creator of the universe. They may believe that salvation is a gift from God. They may believe that salvation is by grace and cannot be earned by works. They may believe that Satan is real and the enemy of God. They may believe that a Christian has a responsibility to share his or her faith in Christ with other people. But still, most believers identify themselves in terms of their names, their jobs, their possessions, or the people they know. If someone were to ask them who they were, and they did not even mention Jesus or the kingdom in their answer, their answer might be an indication that something vital is missing in their self-understanding. If they identify themselves as Christians, but their actions are not consistent with their self-identity, something is not right.

From teaching Christian discipleship and kingdom living in many congregations over the past twenty years in the various Baptist Associations in Upstate South Carolina, it is evident that many people understand more about the institution of the church than they do about the individual call to discipleship. They know more about what the constitution and bylaws of their church says than they do about what the word of God says about their responsibility as disciples. Many leaders in those churches do not understand what it means to be a disciple in God's kingdom. They know how to rule by the world's standards, but not in humility. They believe that the church and the members belong to them. They believe that the pastors work for them and they get to tell the pastors what to do. The result of all of this is that the church members are not growing spiritually or relationally. There is a lot of anger and bitterness at church conferences, and the lack of love is evident. In addition, some churches are not growing numerically because younger members don't feel welcome when visiting the church and many young people who grew up in those churches leave because they feel they are not needed.

The root of the problem is that many churches have members who have not matured in their Christian disciples.

The root of the problem is that many churches have members who have not matured in their Christian disciples. They are disciples by way of salvation, but have not yet matured in their Christian faith. Therefore, many churches are dying because the members do not understand what it means to be a disciple and their role in the discipleship process. They do not clearly understand the great commission that Jesus gave to believers: "Go therefore and make disciples of all the nations, baptizing them in the name of the Father and of the Son and of the Holy Spirit, teaching them to observe all things that I have commanded you; and lo, I am with you always, even to the end of the age. Amen" (Matthew 28:19-20). There is a need for church members to understand for themselves what it means to be a disciple so that they may be effective in making disciples. How can people make disciples if they are not disciples themselves? In Jim Putman's book, *Real-Life Discipleship: Building Churches That Make Disciples,* he says, "When people aren't mature disciples, they cannot value making mature disciples because they don't understand what one looks like."[10] There is a need for believers to understand discipleship if churches are going to see members experience spiritual growth in the twenty-first century.

For years believers have accepted the great commission as their marching order to evangelize the world – to seek and to save—but the salvation of others is only part of the great commission. Let's examine the process of the great commission.

---

[10] Jim Putman, *Real-Life Discipleship: Building Churches That Make Disciples* (Colorado Springs: Nav-Press, 2010), 168.

Believers are to go into all the "world' and "make disciples." The Greek word for world is *kosmos*. The Vine's Expository Dictionary of NT Words defines *kosmos* as "primarily order, arrangement, ornament, adornment; the present condition of human affairs in alienation from and opposition to God."[11] It is where we get the English word cosmos (the universe seen as a well-ordered whole). In essence, *kosmos* is an ordered system of combined activities, affairs, advantages, and accumulated assets of the people on the earth. As believers, we are to go into this lost world that leaves God out and make disciples.

Believers are called to help a person become a disciple of Jesus Christ. In making disciples, believers are not trying to make duplicates of themselves. This would be a boring world if disciples made duplicates of themselves. This world does not need clones, but more people who look more like Jesus. In Bill Hull's book, *The Complete Book on Discipleship,* he says, "Making disciples has nothing to do with winning others over to a philosophy or turning them into nice people who smile a lot. Rather the great commission launches a rescue mission; all followers receive orders with full authority to take action wherever they happen to be."[12] We don't produce, duplicate or create anything. The apostle Paul wrote, "I planted, Apollos

---

[11] W. Vine, *"World - Vine's Expository Dictionary of New Testament Words,"* Blue Letter Bible. 24 Jun, 1996. Web. 31 Jan, 2021. Internet available at: https://www.blueletterbible.org/search/dictionary/viewtopic.cfm.

[12] Bill Hull, *The Complete Book on Discipleship* (Colorado Springs: Navpress, 2006), 26.

watered, but God gave the increase" (1 Corinthians 3:6). To borrow from Christopher B. Adsit, "God is running the show. We are tools in His hands – nothing more, nothing less. Some would-be disciple makers have missed that point and have tried to set themselves up as gurus, expecting the commitment and obedience that is reserved for the Lord Jesus Christ".[13] People who accept Jesus Christ as personal Savior are called Christians. Once people accept Jesus Christ as personal Savior, they begin the discipleship process. In Christianity, a *disciple* means to be a follower of Jesus. The term "disciple" is only found in the New Testament in the Gospels and Acts. In the ancient world, a *disciple* was a follower or adherent of a teacher. It is not the same as being a student in the modern sense. A disciple in the ancient biblical world actively imitated both the life and teaching of the master. Discipleship was a deliberate apprenticeship which made the fully formed disciple a living copy of the master. Jesus said, "A disciple is not above his teacher, nor a slave above his master. It is enough for the disciple that he become as his teacher, and the slave his master" (Matthew 10:24-25). Tony Evans gives a historical picture of the word *disciple*, and what it means to the New Testament believer today:

---

[13] Christopher B. Adsit, *Personal Discipleship: A Step-by-Step Guide for Leading a Christian from New Birth to Maturity* (Orlando: Integrated Resources, 1998), 13.

The word *disciple* means "learner, student." The ancient Greeks had disciples in the realm of philosophy. Plato, often called the "father of philosophy," developed a system of thought that dealt with issues of epistemology, and issues related to the meaning of life. Plato discipled his student Aristotle, who took what he had learned and built "gymnasiums," or academies. In the ancient world, gymnasiums were not arenas for sporting events. They were training centers to teach students Plato's thought and the system developed by Aristotle, known as Aristotelian logic. The students thus trained were "gymnatized," which is the verb form of the Greek word for gymnasium. So successful was this discipling process that it allowed the Greeks to influence the whole Greco-Roman world. This process was called "Hellenization," in which people who were not Greek began to adopt Greek thinking, language, and culture. That was all part of this concept of discipleship. The New Testament picked up this concept and put it in a spiritual context so we would know what it means to be a disciple of Jesus Christ. Discipleship involves an apprenticeship in which the apprentice, or student, is brought toward a particular goal. The word *disciple* itself means "learner." It refers to a student who follows the teachings and pattern of another so closely that the student becomes a "clone" of the teacher, to use a modern-day term. We could also call a disciple an apprentice, someone who stands at the side of a skilled master in a trade to learn that trade thoroughly.[14]

The believer must reach people for the gospel of Jesus Christ and then teach them to become mature disciples. In the great commission (Matthew 28:19-20), the two words "all nations" give us an insight as to whom Jesus was giving the great commission – the church as a corporate body, for it would be impossible for an individual to reach all nations. The second part of the process is "baptizing them in the name of the Father, and of the Son, and of the Holy Ghost" (Matthew 28:19b). The church must admit disciples by the sacred ordinance of baptism, by washing them with water (dipping, pouring or sprinkling). The authority of this baptism is from the three Persons of the Godhead and must be administered in the name of the Father, and of the Son, and of the Holy Spirit. The third part of the process is to teach and develop Christians: "Teaching them to observe all things, whatsoever I have commanded you" (Matthew 28:20a). Here the word *teach*, *didasko* in the Greek, means to give instruction. Jesus's command takes into account every aspect of a person's life, including not just spiritual dimensions, but also daily, practical dimensions, as well. In summary. the great commission is more than a single

---

[14] Tony Evans. (n.d.). "The Process of Discipleship," Accessed December 15, 2020. Internet available at: https://tonyevans.org/the-process-of-discipleship/

command to evangelize the world. It is a process by which we evangelize, identify those who are lost sinners, and witness to them in a step-by-step process of accepting Christ.

The second key description of what it means to be a disciple is found in Matthew 4:19: "And He said to them, 'Follow me, and I will make you fishers of men'" (ESV). Bobby Harrington and Josh Patrick speak eloquently about why this verse is important to discipleship:

> You can easily divide this verse so that it becomes a framework for the three key parts we find in the rest of the New Testament on what it means to be a disciple. These three parts include (1) "following" Jesus (head); (2) "being changed" by Jesus through the Holy Spirit (heart); and (3) being committed to the mission of Christ "fishers of men" (hands). Based on those three parts, check out our definition: A disciple is following Jesus, being changed by Jesus and committed to the mission of Jesus. We always come back to this definition when we talk about disciples. If the people are following Jesus, being changed by Jesus, and committed to the mission of Jesus, then they are biblical disciples, as we understand it. Clarity on these points is essential for disciple makers and churches.

People cannot be disciples of the King until they first enter His realm. They must be born again. In Colossians 1:13-14, Paul wrote, "For He (Christ) delivered us from the domain of darkness, and transferred us to the kingdom of His beloved Son, in whom we have redemption, the forgiveness of sins." A person enters into this new domain by accepting Jesus Christ as Lord and Savior. Jesus said to Nicodemus, "Most assuredly, I say to you, unless one is born again, he cannot see the kingdom of God" (John 3:3). Getting into God's kingdom requires a new spiritual birth. Neil Cole wrote, "Christians are called to the greatest mission in human history—the freedom and salvation of those who are drowning in the bondage of evil. In a very real sense, we are on a search and rescue team sent to find those who are drowning and bring them hope and life, the same hope and life that we have received. We are all called to be kingdom heroes to this generation."

Upon conversion, having moved from darkness to light, believers are baptized and identified with the local church. The process continues as the church helps them become Christ-like by teaching them the Bible. In order for the church to fulfill the great commission, a broad spectrum of talents, gifts, and abilities is required. God has given the church that spectrum in the many different, gifted individuals who can excel in the various areas required to fulfill the process of the great commission.

Discipleship is the process by which a disciple brings all of life under the Lordship of Jesus Christ.

Discipleship is the process by which a disciple brings all of life under the Lordship of Jesus Christ. It cannot be accomplished all at once, any more than a baby can become an adult overnight. How does one become a disciple? To become a disciple of Jesus is not by human effort or man's achievement. Both God and the individual play their respective roles before that individual becomes a disciple of Jesus Christ. Jesus says, "Then Jesus said to those Jews who believed Him, if you abide in My word, you are My disciples indeed" (John 8:31). It takes believing and obeying to become a disciple of Jesus. It takes God's calling for any person to come to Jesus. Jesus said this: "No man can come to me, except the Father which hath sent me draw him and I will raise him up at the last day" (John 6:44). The Scriptures make it so plain that it is God who calls a person to come to Jesus. Jesus Himself emphasized this truth again and again. Thus, to become a disciple, God has to call a person first. A person cannot come by themselves. The subject of Divine calling into discipleship is further made clear when Jesus Christ once said to His disciples: "You did not choose Me, but I chose you and appointed you that you should go and bear fruit, and that your fruit should remain..." *(John 15:16)*.

Becoming a disciple is a lifelong process. The goal of discipleship is conformity to the Savior, being transformed into the image or likeness of Christ. Steve Murrell says, "Discipleship isn't supposed to be complicated. If modern discipleship is confusing and complicated, it is because we have strayed from biblical principles and the simple biblical process that Jesus lived and taught his disciples."[15] Individual disciples may not be where they want to be in their spiritual growth, but each year, they should have grown spiritually beyond where they were the previous year. A disciple should be growing, the way children grow and mark their growth on a chart. Greg Ogden wrote, "If I were Satan and wanted to fatally stunt the growth of disciples to maturity, what would I do? I would divert the leaders from fulfilling their God-given function of equipping the saints. Instead, I would distract them with other good and high-sounding activities that have nothing to do with growing people to maturity and engaging them in ministry. This is exactly what has happened. We have stunted our spiritual leaders into being program developers, administrators and caregivers."[16]

---

[15] Steve Murrell, *WikiChurch: Making Discipleship Engaging, Empowering and Viral* (Lake Mary: Charisma House, 2011), 207.

[16] Greg Ogden, *Transforming Discipleship: Making Disciples a Few at a Time* (Downers Grove: IVP, 2003), 41.

Dietrich Bonhoeffer's wrote, "Christianity without the living Christ is inevitably Christianity without discipleship, and Christianity without discipleship is always Christianity without Christ. It remains an abstract idea, a myth which has a place for the Fatherhood of God, but omits Christ as the living Son."[17] Paul wrote, "For whom He foreknew, He also predestined to be conformed to the image of His Son, that He might be the firstborn among many brethren" (Romans 8:29). Discipleship means to so pattern a believer's life after Christ, to follow Him so closely, that the believer speaks, acts, and thinks like Him.

Disciples are those who line up each area of their lives with Jesus Christ. If they are not careful, they can line up with the wrong object. In Matthew 16:21-23 there is an example of Peter lining up with the wrong object. In verse 21, Jesus predicts that He must go to Jerusalem, suffer many things from the elders, chief priest and scribes, and be resurrected on the third day. In verses 22-23, Peter responds: "Then Peter took Him aside and began to rebuke Him, saying, "Far be it from You, Lord; this shall not happen to You!" But He turned and said to Peter, "Get behind Me, Satan! You are an offense to Me, for you are not mindful of the things of God, but the things of men." Peter was sincere, but he was sincerely wrong.

---

[17] Bonhoeffer, 63-64.

Disciples who disagree with Jesus are wrong. If their interest clashes with His, then they need to change their interest.

In the church, the goal of kingdom discipleship is to present everyone complete in Christ. Paul wrote, "Him we preach, warning every man and teaching every man in all wisdom, that we may present every man perfect in Christ Jesus" (Colossians 1:28). It is not the church's job to make disciples look good, but to make them look more like Jesus. Robby Gallaty wrote, "Disciple Making: Intentionally equipping believers with the Word of God through accountable relationships, empowered by the Holy Spirit, in order to replicate faithful followers of Christ."[18] Steve Murrell wrote that there "are three levels of relationship that must be developed in the discipleship process: relationship with Jesus, relationship with unbelievers, and relationship with believers. The more we celebrate all three relationships, the more we will build a healthy discipleship culture."[19] The Bible tells us to be clothed with Christ. Paul wrote, "For as many of you as were baptized into Christ have put on Christ" (Galatians 3:27). As disciples, we are called to bring even the nations under the Lordship of Jesus Christ.

Being a disciple in the discipleship process demands spiritual growth. The process of spiritual growth is from the inside

---

[18] Robby Gallaty, *Growing Up: How to Be a Disciple Who Makes Disciples* (Bloomington: Crossbooks, 2013), 19.
[19] Murrell, 209.

out. In First Thessalonians 5:23, Paul wrote, "Now may the God of peace Himself sanctify you completely; and may your whole spirit, soul, and body be preserved blameless at the coming of our Lord Jesus Christ." Evan's wrote:

This is the essence of discipleship: As the Holy Spirit empowers the human spirit, the human spirit transforms the soul (personality). The transformed soul then transforms the activity of the body, thus conforming the person's conduct to the image of Christ. God has provided four key resources to help disciples in this process:

1. The Bible provides the authoritative objective truth to govern our choices and decision-making.
2. The Holy Spirit empowers Christians to accomplish the demands of scripture as believers live "under the influence," or "full of the spirit" (Ephesians 5:18), which is accomplished as we make worship a lifestyle and not just an event.
3. Then God uses trials to reveal to us our strengths and weaknesses so that we can tangibly see the areas that still need work. Trials, while painful, are like a good surgeon's knife, always designed to make us better.

4. And finally, God gives us relationships so that the spiritual passion of others keeps us spiritually on fire so that the discipleship process is kept on track.

The result of these divine provisions is conformity to the image of Christ, demonstrated by the reflection of the fruit of the Spirit in the life of the disciple.[20]

Paul wrote, "But the fruit of the Spirit is love, joy, peace, forbearance, kindness, goodness, faithfulness, gentleness and self-control. Against such things there is no law" (Galatians 5:22-23). The word *fruit* is not plural, but singular. In other words, it is expected that disciples should display all of these characteristics at the same time. In addition, the provision of relationships is very important. Putman notes, "Without relationship between believers, there is no model to follow, no authenticity, no accountability, no application, and no support for the journey. These things come through personal contacts. And because that relational context for learning is lacking, life change is much rarer than it should be among Christians today."[21]

There is a discipline to discipleship if believers want to receive the full benefits of the kingdom. Paul wrote, "Have nothing to do with worldly fables fit only for old women. On

---

[20] Evans, *What A Way To Live,* 112-113.
[21] Putman, 22-23.

the other hand, discipline yourself for the purpose of godliness; for bodily discipline is only for a little profit, but godliness is profitable for all things, since it holds promise for the present life and also for the life to come" (1 Timothy 4:7-8). If believers are not exercising themselves spiritually, they are not going to be in great spiritual shape. Spiritual shape comes by discipline that transforms both this life and the life to come.

Spiritual discipline is built into the grace of God. Paul wrote, "For the grace of God has appeared, bringing salvation to all men, instructing us to deny ungodliness and worldly desires and to live sensibly, righteously and godly in the present age, looking for the blessed hope and the appearing of the glory of our great God and Savior, Christ Jesus" (Titus 2:11-13). The basic definition of God's *grace* is the undeserved favor of God. It is God doing for us what we could not do for ourselves. Paul said the grace of God "has appeared." That means it's here. So, when a person says that "I am not a disciplined person" that's all right because grace has taken care of that. Grace will supply the discipline we need. With God's grace, He supplies whatever believers lack in order to get them where He wants them to go. God has already taken their limitations and humanity into account in supplying them with His grace. He knows their weakness and has already calculated that in. They can discipline themselves. So, when a disciple says, "I can't," God has graced them with a supply of spiritual energy to say no to sin and unrighteousness and yes to righteousness. It is the Holy Spirit's job to mediate to disciples the measure of grace they need to move them along toward spiritual maturity as they live in dependence on God. The Holy Spirit is a built-in "power pack" who enables and empowers them to become what God saved them to be. Dodson notes, "The Spirit is the motivation behind the motivation, the personal presence of God's power inclining us to believe the gospel. As it turns out, the gospel is not enough. We desperately need the Spirit to have affection for Christ, to believe his promises, to heed his warnings, to repent from our sin, and to trust Jesus. Without the Spirit, we cannot believe the gospel."[22]

The Spirit's very presence within a disciple is another provision and expression of grace. Gallaty notes that, "With any spiritual discipline, practice moves us from Duty, to Devotion, and ultimately to Delight."[23] Donald Whitney wrote, "I will maintain that the only road to Christian maturity and Godliness (a biblical term synonymous with Christlikeness and holiness) passes through the practice of Spiritual Disciplines."[24]

Many people today want cheap grace. They want the inexhaustible grace of God, but they do not want it to cost them anything. They flock to churches that will allow them to receive

---

[22] Jonathan K. Dodson, Gospel-Centered Discipleship (Wheaton: Crossway, 2012), 101.

[23] Gallaty, 158

[24] Donald S. Whitney, *Spiritual Disciplines for the Christian Life* (Colorado Springs: Navpress, 1991), 16-17.

all of God's blessings without requiring anything of them. Bonhoeffer calls it "grace without price; grace without cost!"[25] In this twenty-first century many people do not want to be convicted of sin. They do not want to be held accountable for their actions. They want God, but on their terms. Bonhoeffer further states, "Cheap grace means the justification of sin without the justification of the sinner. Grace alone does everything, they say, and so everything can remain as it was before. 'All for sin could not atone.' The world goes on in the same old way, and we are still sinners 'even in the best life' as Luther said."[26] Many people feel that since God's grace is sufficient, there is nothing else for them to do. Therefore, they can continue to live like the world because God has done it all for them through His Son. This is the kind of grace that believers bestow upon themselves. It is not a grace from God. A local preacher once said, "In this day and time, it is amazing that anyone truly gets saved." Lifestyles that would have been truly frowned upon just a few years ago are widely accepted as normal today among Christian people. In fact, if someone speaks against such sinful behavior, he or she would be labeled intolerant. Bonhoeffer gives the believer a solution for the twenty-first century. He says, "Yet it is imperative for the Christian to achieve renunciation, to practice self-effacement, to

---

[25] Bonhoeffer, 45.
[26] Ibid., 46.

distinguish his life from the life of the world. He must let grace be grace indeed, otherwise he will destroy the world's faith in the free gift of grace."[27] If this world is going to change, it will be because believers are not only saved by grace, but also practice their faith as obedient disciples. And as obedient disciples they must continue to grow in spiritual maturity. "God freely provides His grace for every contingency and activity in the believers' life, but that grace must be appropriated by choosing to do the work necessary to cultivate spiritual growth."[28] Bonhoeffer sums it up when he says, "Cheap grace is the preaching of forgiveness without requiring repentance, baptism without church discipline, Communion without confession, absolution without personal confession. Cheap grace is grace without discipleship, grace without the cross, grace without Jesus Christ, living and incarnate."[29]

> *The reason so many Christians are struggling with spiritual discipline is because they are doing a program rather than pursuing a Person.*

The reason so many Christians are struggling with spiritual discipline is because they are doing a program rather than

---

[27] Ibid., 46.
[28] Whitney, 116.
[29] Bonhoeffer, 47.

pursuing a Person. When they read their Bibles and pray because that's what good Christians ought to do, they are just fulfilling a program. If they go to church every Sunday just to ensure that they clocked in, they are fulfilling a program. But Jesus didn't die for a program, and neither is a program the Savior. What they should be looking forward to is the appearing of Jesus Christ, not the completion of a program. When they have a passion for the person of Jesus Christ, they won't have a problem with the program. If disciples pursue Jesus Christ as a Person they love, they won't have any problems with the program.

THE DEMANDS OF DISCIPLESHIP

Disciples in the kingdom of God are called to meet certain demands. Many Christians don't really want a personal relationship with the Savior. They just want Him to bring them the goodies. Some Christians only love Christ because of what He can supply. Jesus said, "Behold, I stand at the door and knock. If anyone hears My voice and opens the door, I will come in to him and dine with him, and he with Me" (Revelation 3:20).

The first demand of discipleship is putting Jesus first.

The first demand of discipleship is putting Jesus first. There are three very important Scriptures to help us understand this demand. The first is Deuteronomy 6:4-5: "Hear, O Israel: The LORD our God, the Lord *is* one! You shall love the LORD your God with all your heart, with all your soul, and with all your strength." The second is found in the New Testament and this passage is known as the great commandment: "You shall love the LORD your God with all your heart, with all your soul, and with all your mind" (Matthew 22:37). True disciples are going to the love God with every fabric of their beings. The kind of love that Jesus is talking about here is *agape* love. *Agape* love is an unconditional love. Believers are to love God unconditionally with all their heart, soul and mind. There should be no other God before Him. To love God is to love Him because He is Savior, Creator, Owner, Ruler, and Redeemer. Believers should conduct themselves in love, obedience and dependence on Him. In the Old Testament there were some who made the sun and the moon their gods. One of the problems with this first demand in the twenty-first century is that there are so many gods that a person can follow. Many have made money, materialism, and other people their gods; but unless they embrace the God of the Bible as the true and living God, they cannot be His disciples. Our love for God must be sincere, and not in word only, but in deeds. The third is John 14:15, Jesus said: "If you love me, you will obey my commandments." Mathew Henry notes, "Our love for God must be a singular and superlative love, we must love Him more than anything else; this way the stream of our love must entirely run. The heart must be united to love God, in opposition to a divided heart."[30]

Jesus said, "But seek first the kingdom of God and His righteousness, and all these things shall be added to you" (Matthew 6:33). Many Christians have left their first love (Revelation 2:4). God demands that He be first in everything (Colossians 1:18). Many of God's people are spiritually anemic because Christ is not first in their lives. They will fit Him in when they have time. If Christ is not first, they lose Him in terms of intimate fellowship. They cannot have the victory He supplies, or the power He offers, unless He is first. Once when Jesus called a man to follow Him, the man replied, "Lord, let me first go and bury my father." Jesus said to him, "Allow the dead to bury their own dead, but you go and preach the kingdom of God" (Luke 9:59-60). The proper interpretation of this Scripture is that the father is not dead. The father hasn't died yet. The young man is not saying his father is dead, but that he wants to go home until his father is dead. He wants to bury his father first. When Jesus said, "Let the dead bury their own dead," He may have meant, "Let the spiritually dead bury the physically dead." Let those who don't know God spend their time taking

---

[30] Matthew Henry, *Matthew Henry Commentary* (Peabody: Hendrickson Publishers, Inc., 1991), 263.

care of folk who die, because disciples of Jesus Christ have more to do with the rest of their lives than waiting around for people to die. Jesus wanted people to go out and tell people how to live, not hang around waiting for them to die. Jesus was saying that He had a kingdom job for His disciples to do, that He wanted them to exchange their plans for His. So, what are the implications for the twenty-first century? What are people waiting for before they get serious about God? Are they waiting for the children to grow up and leave? Are they waiting until after they have established their own families or after they have gone to college to follow Jesus? Are they waiting to get their business up and running? Are they waiting until they finish school? Are they waiting until they get out of debt, or they get this weight of economic pressure off of them before they get involved, before they give, before they serve Jesus? Alive people don't talk like that. Spiritually alive disciples understand that Jesus Christ takes priority over all their plans. Jesus wants to be unconditionally first and foremost in the disciple's life.

The second demand of discipleship is a transcending relationship.

The second demand of discipleship is a transcending relationship. Jesus must be so important to disciples that He transcends their most intimate relationships. Jesus said, "If anyone comes to Me and does not hate his father and mother, wife and children, brothers and sisters, yes, and his own life also, he cannot be My disciple" (Luke 14:26). Jesus wants to be more important to disciples than they are to themselves. They must hate their own lives. This means that Jesus wants to be first. He was not talking about literally hating people. He was talking about disciples' decisions. The idea is that when they put their love for Jesus next to their love for anyone else, there should be such a big difference that the other love looks like hate. This is a serious demand because Jesus wants to know that when they have to choose between Him and everybody else, everyone else loses. On one occasion, someone approached Jesus and said, "Lord, I will follow you, but let me first go and bid them farewell, who are at my house" (Luke 9:61). In reflecting on that approach, Bonhoeffer wrote, "He wants to follow, but feels obliged to insist on his own terms. Discipleship to him is a possibility which can only be realized when certain conditions have been fulfilled. This is to reduce discipleship to the level of the human understanding."[31] Jesus responded, "No man, having put his hand to the plough, and looking back, is fit for the kingdom of God." Jesus is dealing

---

[31] Bonhoeffer, 66.

with the influences in a person's life that may change his or her mind. In essence, Jesus is saying that those who start following Him and look back are not fit for Him, because they are going to cut a crooked furrow, and never arrive at the place He wants them to go. This is important for Christian discipleship in the twenty-first century because there are personal influences in people's lives that can be barriers to where God is leading them to go. Disciples must make personal discipleship decisions based on where God is leading them to go. Jesus is instructing disciples to follow Him because if they don't look straight ahead, they are going to mess up. They cannot allow their friends, family, co-workers, school buddies or anybody else to turn them back because they do not know where God's taking them.

The third demand of discipleship is for Jesus to be more important to disciples than their own comfort.

The third demand of discipleship is for Jesus to be more important to disciples than their own comfort. Jesus said, "And whoever does not bear his cross and come after Me cannot be My disciple" (Luke 14:27). Disciples must carry their own crosses, not Jesus' cross. Jesus has taken care of His own. For disciples to carry their own crosses is to bear the reproach of Jesus Christ. It is to be identified with Him and to plead guilty when they accused of being Christians. To carry their own cross is to admit publicly that they are guilty of the crime of being committed to Christ, guilty of placing Him first. It's not comfortable to carry a cross. When disciples admit to the "crime" of being a committed Christian, people may want to punish them. They may want to take out their anger against them. That's not comfortable—but Jesus must be more important than comfort. Once when a man told Jesus that he would follow Jesus wherever Jesus went, Jesus replied, "Foxes have holes and birds of the air *have* nests, but the Son of Man has nowhere to lay *His* head" (Luke 9:58). What Jesus is saying to disciples is that discipleship is not only related to following Him in the comfortable things of life. Discipleship includes following Him when they are worse off than the animal kingdom. Discipleship includes following Him when they don't know where there're going to be able to rest their head, when they don't know where they are going to be able nest down for the evening. Are they willing to follow Him in the insecure places of life? Are they willing to follow Him when He does not tell them ahead of time how it's going to work out? Are they willing to follow Him simply because He's God? Discipleship means that disciples are simply going to follow Him. It means to follow Him when He does not give them the assurances they are seeking. God wants to be unconditionally first, even when it means they are going to have to become uncomfortable. Unfortunately, in the twenty-first century, many believers are following Christ for what they can get out of Him rather than how they can be more like Him. They like to follow Jesus for the goodies. They want their lives to be as comfortable as possible and at the same time claim to follow Him.

The fourth demand of discipleship is that Jesus must be more important than a disciple's possessions.

The fourth demand of discipleship is that Jesus must be more important than a disciple's possessions. Jesus says, "So likewise, whoever of you does not forsake all that he has cannot be My disciple" (Luke 14:33). Jesus is teaching that disciples must give up things if they become possessions. The problem is not in disciples having possessions. The problem is when the possessions have the disciples. A few years ago, there was a conference in Atlanta on *Marketing Your Church for Growth*. The training was good but the focus was not on Christian discipleship, but on how pastors can grow mega churches for their own benefit. One of the facilitators discussed the benefits of having a mega church such as living in mansions, driving Bentleys and even the possibility of owning private jets. That approach is in sharp contrast with the words of Bonhoeffer, who wrote, "Do not let it be a matter of consequence to you that you have outward prosperity; rather keep your goods quietly, having them as if you had them not. Let not your heart be in your goods."[32]

The fifth demand of discipleship is for believers to lose their minds.

The fifth demand of discipleship is for believers to lose their minds. In a spiritual sense, they must lose their minds and take on the mind of Christ. It is impossible for believers to have the mind of Christ while having minds that are filled with other things. To be the kind of disciples that God wants them to be means they must be willing to give up their attitudes, thoughts and actions so that Christ's attitudes, thoughts and actions become theirs. In Philippians 2:5-11, Paul wrote that believers are to take on the mind of Christ. This passage on the humility of Christ is the high mark of the letter. Paul notes in a few verses the uniqueness of the person and work of Christ, and points out that the disposition and mindset of Christians ought to be the disposition and mindset of Christ.

In Philippians 2:5, the apostle Paul says, "Let this mind be in you, which was also in Christ Jesus." It is a command for

---

[32] Ibid., 88.

disciples to take on the mind of Christ. Disciples are expected to develop the mind of Christ. And since the word "Christian" means "like Christ," they are to be like Christ. Letting the mind of Christ be in them means that they are to think as Christ would think, resulting in behavior typical of Christ. If they have the mind of Christ, they are not going to act different than Christ would act. Paul's command to believers is to lose their minds and take on the mind of Christ. Christians must be Christ-minded. They must be Christ-like in their thoughts, their words, and their deeds. How do Christians do this?

First, they do it by being unselfish. In Philippians 2:6, Paul wrote that Jesus, "being in the form of God, thought it not robbery to be equal with God." In other words, even though Jesus was of the same nature of God, did not think this was something to be exploited to His own advantage. He did not try to take something that was not his. Even though Christ in His pre-incarnate state possessed the essential qualities of God, he did not consider His status of divine equality a prize to be used for His own selfish motives or desires. Instead, He "made himself of no reputation, and took upon him the form of a servant, and was made in the likeness of men" (Philippians 2:7). Christ "emptied Himself" of His divine privileges, but not of His divinity. He imposed upon Himself limitations so He could identify with humankind. He voluntarily waived some of His divine rights during the time He was on earth. He was very much God and man, but He divested, stripped, and emptied himself of the honors and glories of eternity, and of His former appearance, to clothe Himself with the rags of human nature.

Second, disciples become Christ-like by being humble and submissive. Describing Jesus, Paul wrote, "And being found in fashion as a man, he humbled himself, and became obedient unto death, even the death of the cross" (Philippians 2:8). Humility is defined as being "low-lying, of low degree, brought low."[33] The most common Greek word translated "humble" is *tapeinoo,* which means to make low. The word literally means "to level a mountain or a hill." Simply said, humility means being of low estate. It means seeing others as higher than ourselves. Humility is a theme throughout. The prophet Micah wrote, "He has shown you, O man, what *is* good; And what does the LORD require of you But to do justly, To love mercy, And to walk humbly with your God?" (Micah 6:8). James wrote, "But He gives more grace. Therefore, He says: 'God resists the proud, But gives grace to the humble' . . . "Humble yourselves in the sight of the Lord, and He will lift you up" (James 4:6, 10). And one of most profound Scriptures is found in 2 Chronicles 7:14: "If my people, which are called by my name, shall humble themselves, and pray, and seek my face,

---

[33] Vines, W. E., M. A. "Entry for 'Humble'. Vine's Expository Dictionary of NT Words," https://www.studylight.org/dictionaries/eng/ved/h/humble.html. 1940.

and turn from their wicked ways; then will I hear from heaven, and will forgive their sin, and will heal their land." Jesus has set the standards for humility. Besides submitting Himself to the worst dethronement in history, Christ yielded Himself to ridicule, arrest, mockery, beatings, and finally death on the cross. If believers want to know how much Jesus loves them, they need look no further than the cross. Jesus gave up His throne in Heaven to submit Himself to the most excruciating and dehumanizing form of human punishment. In this twenty-first century, believers must humble themselves if they want God to do a great work in their lives.

Third, disciples become Christ-like with an attitude of sacrifice. Because of His unconditional love for the world and His loyalty to the Father, He lived and died sacrificially, thereby achieving victory over death by the power of God. Disciples of Jesus Christ should make sacrifices for the same reasons. As noted earlier in Romans 12:1, believers are called to present their bodies as a "living sacrifice."

True disciples in the twenty-first century will be required to make sacrifices, live holy lives in obedience to Christ, and be transformed from the world's way of thinking to God's way of thinking.

True disciples in the twenty-first century will be required to make sacrifices, live holy lives in obedience to Christ, and be transformed from the world's way of thinking to God's way of thinking. All of these requirements can only be fulfilled by the Holy Spirit's power at work in the lives of believers.

THE CALLING OF DISCIPLESHIP

Finally, the calling of discipleship is a divine mission which God has ordained for His disciples and burned into their hearts. God equips disciples to accomplish His mission in the world and to advance the kingdom. A divine calling always has to do with God's glory, with fulfilling His kingdom agenda. If disciples are not advancing God's kingdom and bringing Him glory, they have not yet found their calling.

First, the calling of discipleship is a customized calling. It is uniquely designed to help them reflect God's purpose for their lives. This is why disciples must "work out their own salvation with fear and trembling" (Philippians 2:12). A disciple does not have to copy someone else's calling. God did not design individual disciples to be like anyone else. Rick Warren wrote, "You're not saved by service, but you are saved for service. In God's kingdom, you have a place, a purpose, a role, and a function to fulfill. This gives your life great significance and value."[34] God has customized the calling of all disciples so that

---

[34] Rick Warren, *The Purpose Driven Life* (Grand Rapids: Zondervan, 2002), 228.

when they come to the end of their lives, they can say that they have finished the work God gave them to do. Near the end of His life, Jesus said, "I have glorified You on the earth. I have finished the work which You have given Me to do" (John 17:4).

Second, a disciples' calling involves more than a job or career. Paul was a tentmaker, yet his calling was to preach the Word. The calling of discipleship involves everything that God has in mind for disciples to bring Him glory and expand His kingdom. God gave Adam the calling to have dominion over the rest of creation, but Adam had some specific tasks to fulfill such as tending the garden and naming the animals. In Exodus 3:1-4 Moses had an encounter with God:

> Now Moses was tending the flock of Jethro his father-in-law, the priest of Midian. And he led the flock to the back of the desert, and came to Horeb, the mountain of God. And the Angel of the LORD appeared to him in a flame of fire from the midst of a bush. So he looked, and behold, the bush was burning with fire, but the bush *was* not consumed. Then Moses said, "I will now turn aside and see this great sight, why the bush does not burn." So when the LORD saw that he turned aside to look, God called to him from the midst of the bush and said, "Moses, Moses!" And he said, "Here I am."

Tony Evans wrote, "If you want to find your calling, look for God. When you find God, His calling will find you. God's calling for your life, then, will be experienced out of your relationship with Him. If there is no relationship, you will not come to know what your calling is all about."[35] Moses met God at a burning bush because he came to the mountain of God. Disciples won't find their calling if they never have time to go before the face of God, or never find time to spend in His Word, or never have the time to be around the people of God. When they encounter God, He will lead them to their calling. Their calling will find them when they find God.

Third, the Person of God comes before the call of God. God was about to give Moses his calling. But Moses did not get God's program until he responded to God's Person. Relationship precedes the calling. Evan further states, "It's not enough to get on your knees and say, 'Lord, show me my calling; show me Your program,' when your relationship with Him is in disrepair. If you don't relate to His Person, God won't trust you with His program."[36]

An example of someone putting the Person before the program can be found in Luke 10:38-42:

Now it happened as they went that He entered a certain village; and a certain woman named Martha welcomed Him

---

[35] Evans, *What A Way To Live*, 129.
[36] Ibid., 130.

into her house. And she had a sister called Mary, who also sat at Jesus' feet and heard His word. But Martha was distracted with much serving, and she approached Him and said, "Lord, do You not care that my sister has left me to serve alone? Therefore, tell her to help me." And Jesus answered and said to her, "Martha, Martha, you are worried and troubled about many things. But one thing is needed, and Mary has chosen that good part, which will not be taken away from her.

Martha and Mary invited Jesus into their home. Mary was sitting at Jesus' feet. Martha, distracted by much serving (her program), got upset and blamed Jesus for her sister not helping her. Jesus said to Martha, "Only one thing is needful, and Mary has chosen that good part, which will not be taken away from her" (Luke 10:42). Mary had chosen to make Jesus more important than Martha's cooking program. Jesus was saying that a personal relationship with Him is better than the program. Jesus wants a personal relationship with His disciples before He is willing to give them His program. Many people are doing some great work for the Lord, but the work is out of order. Christ should be the priority over any work that is done. Believers can be so involved in the work of the church that they forget the Person of the church. Twenty-first century disciples cannot allow the work of the church to distract them from the Person of Jesus Christ.

In Exodus 3, God called Moses by name, and Moses's call came out of a personal commitment. In his letter to the Romans, Paul wrote, "I beseech you therefore, brethren, by the mercies of God, that you present your bodies a living sacrifice, holy, acceptable to God, which is your reasonable service. And do not be conformed to this world, but be transformed by the renewing of your mind, that you may prove what is that good and acceptable and perfect will of God" (Romans 12:1-2). In the twenty-first century, many believers are being conformed to this world far more than being transformed into the likeness of Christ. Paul is saying that, if believers are going to know God's will for their lives, and their calling in the kingdom, they must be transformed by the renewing of their minds. Paul wrote, "Present your bodies a living sacrifice," but how can disciples be living sacrifices? Sacrifices were put to death! In this letter to the Galatians, Paul answered that question: "I am crucified with Christ; and it is no longer I who live, but Christ lives in me; and the life which I now live in the flesh I live by faith in the Son of God, who loved me, and delivered Himself up for me" (Galatians 2:20). Paul considered himself a living dead person because he was dead to his own life and plans and alive to God's.

Fourth, there is the certainty of a disciple's calling. Jesus said, "My doctrine is not Mine, but His who sent Me. If anyone wills to do His will, he shall know concerning the doctrine, whether it is from God or whether I speak on My own authority" (John 7:16-17). Disciples must be willing to do God's will before they know His will. Many people will say to God, "Show me what You want me to do, and I will let You know whether I am into that or not. Let me know the plan, and I will tell You whether I plan to do it." But God's plan is not up for negotiation. God will not negotiate His will. In keeping with the appeal in Romans 12:1-2, disciples must give all of themselves to God as living sacrifices. If believers conform to this world, God will not reveal His calling for their lives. They must say, as Moses said to God at the burning bush, "Here I am" (Exodus 3:4) or what Isaiah said to God, "Here am I! Send me" (Isaiah 6:8).

When Jesus had called the people to Himself, with His disciples also, He said to them, "Whoever desires to come after Me, let him deny himself, and take up his cross, and follow Me. For whoever desires to save his life will lose it, but whoever loses his life for My sake and the gospel's will save it. For what will it profit a man if he gains the whole world, and loses his own soul?" (Mark 8:34-36). Believers are either saving their lives or losing them. But can believers save their lives, and still lose them? By going after the world's system. They cannot find God's calling for their lives if they are too busy trying to save their lives by gaining the world. Giving themselves totally to God means giving Him full control over their lives. Jesus says the way to find life is to lose it for His sake. When believers do this, God will reveal the calling to them. Bonhoeffer notes that, "To deny oneself is to be aware only of Christ and no more of self, to see only him who goes before and no more the road which is too hard for us. Once more, all that self-denial can say is: He leads the way, keep close to him."[37]

In conclusion, it is important to note that disciples do suffer because of identifying with the cross. Because of the cross, disciples share the burden of Christ's suffering. But the good news is that Christ was victorious over the cross. As the Scripture says in the First Epistle of Peter, "Beloved, do not think it strange concerning the fiery trial which is to try you, as though some strange thing happened to you; but rejoice to the extent that you partake of Christ's sufferings, that when His glory is revealed, you may also be glad with exceeding joy" (1 Peter 4:12-13). In Bonhoeffer's words, "The call to discipleship, the baptism in the name of Jesus Christ means both death and life. The call of Christ, his baptism, sets the Christian in the middle of the daily arena against sin and the devil. Every day he encounters new temptations, and every day he must suffer anew for Jesus Christ's sake."[38] In the next chapter, we will discover the impact of the kingdom of God on discipleship.

---

[37] Bonhoeffer, 97.
[38] Ibid., 99.

CHAPTER TWO

THE IMPACT OF THE KINGDOM OF GOD ON DISCIPLESHIP

The focus of the last chapter was on the meaning of the terms disciple and discipleship. After accepting Jesus Christ as personal Savior, a disciple of Jesus Christ has moved from darkness to the kingdom of light. The marvelous light represents the domain of the kingdom of God, which is in the midst of the disciple. It is important to realize how the kingdom of God impacts every area of a disciple's life. The way Jesus used the word kingdom is different from the common understanding of the word. Today, many people understand kingdom to mean the physical territory or people ruled by a king, or some other governmental figure. In the Gospels, the Pharisees and Sadducees did not understand the kingdom message proclaimed by Jesus. Many were looking for a Messiah who would bring an earthly kingdom, but Jesus was bringing a kingdom that would change human hearts based on His Word. A sad commentary in this twenty-first century is that there are many individual believers and churches who do not understand the kingdom. Many churches are more focused on tradition than on the kingdom. Jesus came to introduce the world to the kingdom of God. Munroe says: "The Kingdom of God is at the center of everything. God's every action and activity is motivated by His desire and passion to see His Kingdom established on the earth."39 In this twenty-first century it is very important for the church to understand the importance of the kingdom of God in the life of the disciple.

> *In this twenty-first century, it is very important for the church to understand the importance of the kingdom of God in the life of the disciple.*

The phrase "kingdom of God" is related to the concepts of king and kingship in the life of Israel. What does the *kingdom* mean? The Greek word for *kingdom* is *basileia*, which means

---

39 Munroe, 197.

basically a "rule" or "authority." It means the sovereignty, reign and rule of God. Included in this definition is the idea of power. In essence, God is king, ruler, and has all power. Therefore, kingdom discipleship refers to disciples submitting to God's reign, rule, and authority in their lives for the purpose of engaging in a relationship with Him. It also refers to the process of discipling others by showing them how to submit to God's reign, rule, and authority in their lives.

> ### *The basic message of Jesus and His disciples in the Gospels was that the kingdom of God was near.*

The basic message of Jesus and His disciples in the Gospels was that the kingdom of God was near. There is no need for an earthly king, because Jesus Christ is now King who will reign over both heaven and earth. In Mark 1:15, Jesus said, "The time is fulfilled, and the kingdom of God is at hand." The phrase "the time is fulfilled" implies that Jesus was the fulfillment of the promise. The kingdom at hand means it is here and now. Jesus taught His disciples how to pray about this kingdom, "In this manner, therefore, pray: Our Father in heaven, hallowed be Your name, Your Kingdom come, Your will be done on earth, as it is in heaven" (Matthew 6:9-10). Munroe says, "The Kingdom of heaven refers to the sovereign presence and authority of God 'invading' and impacting the earthly environment. Jesus challenged His listeners to change from a mindset that ignored or denied God's Kingdom to one that acknowledged and embraced its arrival."[40] Evans makes this comment about the kingdom: "Throughout the Bible, the Kingdom of God is His rule, His plan, His program. God's Kingdom is all-embracing. It covers everything in the universe. In fact, we can define God's Kingdom as His comprehensive rule over all creation."[41] In the twenty-first century, the disciple of Jesus Christ must understand that in the Kingdom of God, God rules. The ultimate agenda for the disciple is God's agenda. A disciple may have his or her own plans for life, but those plans must come under the comprehensive rule of God.

Another important word to note is *reign*. The word *reign* means to possess or exercise sovereign power or authority; to rule; to exercise government, as a king or emperor; or to hold the supreme power. An earthly example of reigning is Queen Elizabeth II. She has been reigning for over sixty years, but God has been reigning over the entire world since the beginning of time. In Revelation 11:15, John says, "Then the seventh angel sounded: And there were loud voices in heaven, saying, "The kingdoms of this world have become the kingdoms of our Lord and of His Christ, and He shall reign forever and ever!"

---

[40] Ibid., 120-121.
[41] Tony Evans, *What a Way to Live,* 15.

Andrew Kirk, in his book *The Good News of the Kingdom Coming,* sums up what is involved in the reign of God:

The kingdom sums up God's plan to create a new human life by making possible a new kind of community among people, families and groups. [It combines] the possibility of a personal relationship to Jesus with man's responsibility to manage wisely the whole of nature; the expectation that real change is possible here and now; a realistic assessment of the strength of opposition to God's intentions; the creation of new human relationships and the eventual liberation by God of the whole of nature from corruption.[42]

The terms *king and kingship* are commonly used biblical words. The words designate the person who holds supreme authority of a city or nation. In general, references to *king* and *kingship* in the Old Testament deal with the periods of the united and divided kingdoms of ancient Israel. The kings who ruled over the united Israelite kingdom were Saul, David, and Solomon. When Solomon died, the kingdom was divided into northern (Israel) and southern (Judah) segments. After his death, there was a long succession of kings in both Israel and Judah from 931 until 721 BC in the north and 586 BC in the south. But the use of the terms *king and kingdom* was not limited to the thrones in Samaria and Jerusalem. God's kingship

---

[42] Andrew Kirk, *The Good News of the Kingdom Coming* (Downers Grove: Intervarsity, 1983), 47.

was different from the kingship of Israel's rulers in that God's rule was not limited to the nation of Israel. God's kingship not only included Israel, but extended to all nations and all people. The psalmist said, "The earth is the LORD's, and the fullness thereof; the world, and they that dwell therein" (Psalm 24:1).

In the Old Testament there was a dualism of sovereignty, which presented a major problem for the people of God in the Old Testament period. The covenant people needed to understand their relationship and obligation to their earthly king in light of their relationship and obligation to God. Moreover, in Old Testament times, Israel was surrounded by nations who were also governed by kings. These nations were Assyria, Babylonia, Egypt and the nations of Canaan. The concept of kingship did not apply to Israel until around 1000 BC. Before then, the Bible says, "In those days there was no king in Israel; everyone did what was right in his own eyes" (Judges 21:25). While the twelve tribes enjoyed their independence, they would come together when they were attacking a mutual enemy under the leadership of special leaders and judges chosen by God. Because of the frequency of these attacks, the people demanded a more permanent form of leadership. Finally, in 1 Samuel 8:5, the people said, "Now make us a king to judge us like all the nations."

When Israel said they wanted to be like other nations, they denied their special relationship with God. When God used

Moses to deliver His people, they saw themselves as God's chosen people because they had God on their side. They did not need an earthly king. Samuel warned the people in 1 Samuel 8:11-18 about having an earthly king, but they demanded one anyway. In the end, the Lord allowed the Israelites to have a king. This king would need to be chosen by God and lead the people God's way. The people got their king in King Saul, but God would continue to rule over them.

The Old Testament gives positives and negatives on how this kingship worked for Israel. There were good kings and there were bad kings. For example, when Saul was appointed King, he quickly forgot his role as God's appointed leader. He disobeyed God and was rejected by the people. In fact, "the Lord regretted that He made Saul king over Israel" (1 Samuel 15:35). After Saul, David became king and was "a man after God's own heart" (1 Samuel 13:14). There were several kings after David's lineage who would rule over Israel. Some kings refused to obey God's rules like Ahab and Manasseh, while others like Hezekiah and Josiah did their best to obey and serve God and were rewarded for their faithfulness with many years as king. Israel's kingdom came to an end in 721 B.C. when the northern kingdom (Israel) was destroyed by the Assyrians and the southern kingdom (Judah) was defeated by the Babylonians in 597 BC, when King Zedekiah was taken into captivity.

The prophets were frequently looking for the Lord to visit them in the immediate future, the "day of the Lord," which would be characterized by God's divine wrath on the enemy. Joel prophesied about the day of the Lord in Joel 2:1-2:

Blow the trumpet in Zion, and sound an alarm in My holy mountain! Let all the inhabitants of the land tremble; For the day of the LORD is coming, for it is at hand: A day of darkness and gloominess, A day of clouds and thick darkness, Like the morning clouds spread over the mountains. A people come, great and strong, The like of whom has never been; Nor will there ever be any such after them, Even for many successive generations.

In his book, *Introduction to the Old Testament*, Edward Young wrote, "The prophecy of Joel was fulfilled fully and finally on the day of Pentecost. The fulfillment of this prophecy of grace occurred when the Holy Spirit was poured out at Pentecost (Acts 2:17)."[43] In Amos 5:18-19, the prophet said:

Woe to you who desire the day of the LORD! For what good is the day of the LORD to you? It will be darkness, and not light. It will be as though a man fled from a lion, And a bear met him! Or as though he went into the house, Leaned his hand on the wall, And a serpent bit him! Is not the day of

---

[43] Edward J. Young, *Introduction to the Old Testament* (Grand Rapids: Eerdmans, 1960), 155.

the LORD darkness, and not light? Is it not very dark, with no brightness in it?

In Zephaniah 1:7, the prophet said, "Be silent in the presence of the Lord GOD; For the day of the LORD is at hand, For the LORD has prepared a sacrifice; He has invited His guests." In William Sanford Lasor's book, *Old Testament Survey,* he wrote, "Zephaniah elaborates on Amos's outline of the Day of the Lord, showing just how dark that "day of darkness not light" will be. In a startlingly unique metaphor, the day is likened to a banquet in which those who expect to be guests become victims."[44] In Zechariah 1:14-15, the prophet wrote, "So the angel who spoke with me said to me, 'Proclaim, saying, "Thus says the LORD of hosts: 'I am zealous for Jerusalem And for Zion with great zeal. I am exceedingly angry with the nations at ease; For I was a little angry, And they helped—but with evil intent.'" These Scriptures prophesy doom and gloom for the immediate day of the Lord.

The day of the Lord is also characterized by divine blessings for His people. In Isaiah 4:2-6, the prophet wrote:

In that day the Branch of the LORD will be beautiful and glorious, and the fruit of the land will be the pride and glory of the survivors in Israel. Those who are left in Zion,

---

[44] William Sanford Lasor, *Old Testament Survey* (Grand Rapids: Eerdmans, 1996), 317.

who remain in Jerusalem, will be called holy, all who are recorded among the living in Jerusalem. The LORD will wash away the filth of the women of Zion; he will cleanse the bloodstains from Jerusalem by a spirit of judgment and a spirit of fire. Then the LORD will create over all of Mount Zion and over those who assemble there a cloud of smoke by day and a glow of flaming fire by night; over everything the glory will be a canopy. It will be a shelter and shade from the heat of the day, and a refuge and hiding place from the storm and rain.

The prophet Micah wrote, "In that day," says the LORD, "I will assemble the lame, I will gather the outcast And those whom I have afflicted; I will make the lame a remnant, And the outcast a strong nation; So the LORD will reign over them in Mount Zion From now on, even forever. And you, O tower of the flock, The stronghold of the daughter of Zion, To you shall it come, Even the former dominion shall come, The kingdom of the daughter of Jerusalem" (Micah 4:6-8).

In Amos 9:11-15, the prophet Amos gives a ray of hope for the day of the Lord. On that day, God will bring restoration to the children of Israel by restoring the tabernacle of David. David's kingdom will be restored and the Gentiles will be brought into that restored kingdom. In other words, all the nations on whom the name of Christ is called will be brought into the kingdom of God. Wherever the gospel is preached to the nations, people will come into the kingdom of God. This is a hope for all who are not descendants of Jacob. It is a promise that those outside of Israel will have access to God. Even as His judgment was coming upon Israel and the nations of the ancient world, God promised that out of chaos and calamity He would raise up a place of worship for all who will come to Him. This promise was fulfilled in Christ, who broke down the wall of separation between Jew and Gentile, so that everyone may enter into the grace of God (Ephesians 2:14-22). Christ's kingdom is a spiritual kingdom which will eventually dominate the whole world.

Even as the day of the Lord was a hope for the future kingdom that Jesus was bringing, it is even more of a hope for humankind in this twenty-first century after Jesus's resurrection. There is an assurance that the kingdom of God is here now for everyone who calls upon the name of Jesus. Ladd writes, "An all-important fact in Jesus' proclamation of the Kingdom was the recovery of the prophetic tension between history and eschatology. . . . In this person and mission, the Kingdom of God had come near in history in fulfillment of the prophetic hope; but it would yet come in eschatological consummation in the future at a time known only to God."[45] He further writes, "To the human eye, the world appears little changed; the

---

[45] George Eldon Ladd, *The Presence of the Future* (Grand Rapids: Eerdmans, 1974), 320.

kingdom of Satan is unshaken. Yet the Kingdom of God has come among men; and those who receive it will be prepared to enter into the Kingdom of Glory when Christ comes to finish the good work He has already begun."[46] The day of the Lord will bring both blessings and judgment to a variety of people. It will demonstrate God's sovereign rule, which shows God's wrath and His blessings at the same time. "God is the Lord of history. His lordship is manifested by historical visitations for judgment and deliverance and by an eschatological visitation for final judgment and deliverance . . . The present is viewed in light of the future; and the proclamation of the future visitations of God, both historical and eschatological, are designed to bring God's people into conformity with the divine will in the present."[47]

There is a 400-year gap between the end of the Old Testament period and the beginning of the New Testament period. During this intertestamental period, a variety of kingdom images developed in Jewish apocalyptic literature. The intertestamental period was called the silent years because many believed that during these years no prophet spoke in the land of Israel and no official biblical text was written until the time of John the Baptist. It was almost as if God were silent, but God was not silent. He was paving the way for the coming Messiah. In the

---

[46] Ibid., 50-51.
[47] Ibid., 69.

Gospel of Matthew, John the Baptist was introduced this way: "Now John himself was clothed in camel's hair, with a leather belt around his waist; and his food was locusts and wild honey" (Matthew 3:4). Richard Hughes observed, "In keeping with the values of the kingdom of heaven—or the kingdom of God—Matthew wants us to know that John the Baptist was not clad in imperial regalia. The contrast between John, on the one hand, and Herod and Archelaus on the other— and therefore between the kingdom of God and empire— could hardly be greater."[48] John came speaking to the people with a message of repentance: "Repent, for the Kingdom of God is at hand" (Matthew 3:2). He was calling his contemporaries to get ready for the kingdom of God to come. It was a powerful message and people flocked into the desert of Judea to hear him preach. Some even thought that he was the coming Messiah. But John the Baptist clarified: "I indeed baptize you with water unto repentance, but He who is coming after me is mightier than I, whose sandals I am not worthy to carry. He will baptize you with the Holy Spirit and fire" (Matthew 3:11). For 400 years, there was no one like John the Baptist. And because of the bondage of the Jewish people under the Roman government, his message was welcomed by the Jewish

---

[48] Richard T. Hughes. *"Christian America and the Kingdom of God,"* University of Illinois Press; 2009. Accessed February 7, 2021, 63. Internet available at: http://ezproxy.erskine.edu:2170/login.aspx?direct=true&AuthType=ip,uid&db=nlebk&AN=569613&site=ehost-live&scope=site

people. The hope of the coming Messiah dominated Jewish thinking during this period of time. The Jewish people looked forward to the time when this divinely appointed king would come and assume kingship over Israel and deliver the Jewish people from their oppressors. They were looking forward to a Messiah who would establish the kingdom of God on earth. In Matthew 3, John introduced the world to this Messiah and the Kingdom of God. Many of the Jewish people thought that John was the Messiah, but John was the one crying in the wilderness as prophesized by the prophet Isaiah. John wanted the people to prepare the way for the Lord's coming. His message was a call to repentance, which is the same message that Jesus proclaimed. It is easy to see why the Jewish people flocked to John the Baptist and Jesus.

In Galatians 4:4-5, Paul wrote, "But when the fullness of the time had come, God sent forth His Son, born of a woman, born under the law, to redeem those who were under the law, that we might receive the adoption as sons." That phrase, "the fullness of time," implies that, during the intertestamental period when God was believed to be silent, God was actively working to prepare the world for the coming of the Savior (the Messiah; the Lord Jesus Christ).

There was much apocalyptic literature written in the Jewish community during this intertestamental period. The Jewish people were highly educated, strongly devoted to their culture and the tenets of Judaism (the monotheistic religion of the Jews); as such, they were a well-read people. Jewish apocalyptic literature-maintained stability in the region for the Jewish people during the intertestamental era. The most significant collection of literature during the intertestamental period became known as the Apocrypha. The word *Apocrypha* is from the Greek word *apokrypha*, meaning "the hidden things," although there is no strict sense in which these books are hidden. The *Harper's Bible Dictionary* makes this note about the Apocrypha: "The Apocrypha content reflects the struggle of the Jewish people to maintain faith as they encountered religious, political, and military opposition under foreign rule in Palestine and attempted to preserve their way of life in the face of the power of Hellenistic culture both at home and in the Diaspora (i.e., those lands other than Palestine where Jews lived)".[49]

During the intertestamental period, there was a relationship between messianic expectations and the coming Kingdom. There was an expectation that the Messiah would reign as king over the earth. Jeremiah wrote, "Behold, the days are coming," says the LORD, That I will raise to David a Branch of righteousness; A King shall reign and prosper, And execute judgment and righteousness in the earth. In His days Judah will be saved, And Israel will dwell safely; Now this is His

---

[49] Paul J. Achtemeier, *Harper's Bible Dictionary* (San Francisco: Harper & Row Publishers, 1985), 38.

name by which He will be called: THE LORD OUR RIGHTEOUSNESS" (Jeremiah 23:5-6). In Daniel's vision about the coming kingdom, he says:

> "I was watching in the night visions, And behold, One like the Son of Man, Coming with the clouds of heaven! He came to the Ancient of Days, And they brought Him near before Him. Then to Him was given dominion and glory and a kingdom, That all peoples, nations, and languages should serve Him. His dominion is an everlasting dominion, Which shall not pass away, And His kingdom the one Which shall not be destroyed" (Daniel 7:13-14).

The Jewish people expected a conquering Messiah who would destroy their enemies and restore their land. They were not looking for a heavenly kingdom or freedom from sin. They were looking for their freedom to be restored in Israel, exclusively among the descendants of Abraham.

Jesus's teaching about the kingdom is both similar to and dissimilar from expectations of the kingdom in Judaism. Jesus taught His disciples about God's kingdom and what it looks like. He said, "I must declare the good news of the kingdom of God, because for this I was sent forth" (Luke 4:43). Jesus was sent to introduce humankind to the good news of the kingdom. The central theme of Jesus's teaching was the kingdom of God, and there were several characteristics of the kingdom that Jesus emphasized.

First, Jesus taught that He was the anointed Messiah and King. When the Samaritan woman at the well told Jesus that she knew the Messiah was coming, Jesus said, "I who speak to you am He" (John 4:26). In Matthew 19:28, Jesus told His disciples about his glorious throne: "Assuredly I say to you, that in the regeneration, when the Son of Man sits on the throne of His glory, you who have followed Me will also sit on twelve thrones, judging the twelve tribes of Israel." Jesus not only told them about His glorious throne, but that they too would sit on twelve thrones, judging the twelve tribes of Israel. When Pontius Pilate asked Jesus if He was the king of the Jews, Jesus answered him and said, "It is as you say" (Luke 23:3). In Revelation 19:16, John said, "And on His robe and on His thigh He has a name written, "KING OF KINGS, AND LORD OF LORDS." He is the designated King who sits at the right hand of the Father. He is the sovereign ruler who will reign forever and ever. In this twenty-first century the disciple of Jesus Christ must resolve that Jesus is still the anointed Messiah and King, especially in a time when satanic forces are at work to dismantle the relevance of Jesus. Many religions today are still viewing Jesus as just a good prophet.

Second, Jesus taught that in God's kingdom there is true justice. Unlike the Pharisees who set up barriers that divided people, Jesus brought down the walls that divided us by His life and death. He was no respecter of persons, but demonstrated impartiality daily by teaching men and women, rich and poor, Jew and Gentile. The apostle Paul summarizes it well:

For Christ himself has made peace between us Jews and you Gentiles by making us all one people. He has broken down the wall of hostility that used to separate us. By his death he ended the whole system of Jewish law that excluded the Gentiles. His purpose was to make peace between Jews and Gentiles by creating in himself one new person from the two groups. Together as one body, Christ reconciled both groups to God by means of his death, and our hostility toward each other was put to death. He has brought this Good News of peace to you Gentiles who were far away from him, and to us Jews who were near (Ephesians 2:14-17, NLT).

Jesus wanted everyone to know that the kingdom of God was available to all who seek Him as Lord and Savior. Reading from the scroll of Isaiah, Jesus applied these words to His own mission: "The Spirit of the Lord is upon Me, Because He has anointed Me To preach the gospel to the poor; He has sent Me to heal the brokenhearted, To proclaim liberty to the captives And recovery of sight to the blind, To set at liberty those who are oppressed" (Isaiah 61:1; Luke 4:18). The religious leaders of His day showed bias or favoritism, but Jesus showed no trace of either. He wanted all of humankind to experience the freedom of being a part of the richness of His kingdom. An excellent example of this is in Galatians when Paul confronted Peter about his bias. Peter was eating with the Gentiles, but when His Jewish friend came along, he withdrew from them because he was afraid of criticism from these people who insisted on the necessity of circumcision. As a result of Peter's hypocrisy, other Jews also followed. Paul rebuked Peter by saying, "Since you, a Jew by birth, have discarded the Jewish laws and are living like a Gentile, why are you now trying to make these Gentiles follow the Jewish traditions?" (Galatians 2:14, NLT). In the twenty-first century, the disciple of Jesus Christ must not show bias or favoritism, but act in a way that will bring equality and justice to all humankind. Oppression or prejudice of any kind minimizes the effectiveness of the kingdom of God.

Third, Jesus taught that God's kingdom was not of this world. Jesus did not come on horses and chariot to take over the political kingdoms because His kingdom was not of this world. He was not caught up in the political affairs of that day. The warfare He was fighting was not physical, but spiritual. In fact, "when Jesus perceived that they were about to come and take Him by force to make Him king, He departed again to the mountain by Himself alone" (John 6:15). The people tried to force Him to be king. But Jesus said, "My kingdom is not of this world. If My kingdom were of this world,

My servants would fight, so that I should not be delivered to the Jews; but now My kingdom is not from here" (John 18:36). Jesus even informed His disciples that they were not a part of this world in John 15:19, "If you were of the world, the world would love its own. Yet because you are not of the world, but I chose you out of the world, therefore the world hates you." Jesus did not even allow His disciples to use weapons to defend Him: "And, behold, one of them which were with Jesus stretched out his hand, and drew his sword, and struck a servant of the high priests, and smote off his ear. Then said Jesus unto him, Put up again thy sword into his place: for all they that take the sword shall perish with the sword" (Matthew 26:51). In the twenty-first century, disciples need to understand that this is not their home. The closer they draw to Jesus, the more the world will hate them. The world is not sitting around saying, "Where have you been all my life?" The world is waiting to persecute disciples for embracing the truth of Jesus Christ.

Fourth, Jesus taught that the kingdom of God would be based on love. People were drawn to Jesus because of His love. This was a love that was not based on whether one was deserving of it. It was God's unconditional *agape* love. He was approachable because of His love. Even the marginalized flocked to Him because they knew He would treat them with kindness and dignity. The essence of love in the kingdom of God is found in Matthew 22:37-40: "Jesus said to him, 'you shall love the LORD your God with all your heart, with all your soul, and with all your mind.' This is the first and great commandment. And the second is like it: 'You shall love your neighbor as yourself.' On these two commandments hang all the Law and the Prophets." Love was the test to determine whether a disciple was truly a follower of Jesus Christ. Jesus said, "By this all will know that you are My disciples, if you have love for one another" (John 13:35). In the twenty-first century, the true *agape* love of God must be demonstrated and duplicated in the life of the disciple. John said, "Dear friends, since God so loved us, we also ought to love one another. No one has ever seen God; but if we love one another, God lives in us and his love is made complete in us" (1 John 4:11-12, NIV). This is how love is duplicated among disciples. Disciples who love one another are reflecting the very love of God. And this is how others will see God's love. While the demonstration of His love through the death of His Son Jesus Christ is a bold fact of history, many people will never look at that historical fact until they see God's love manifested in the lives of disciples. The world is looking at the disciple for evidence that there is a God of love.

An excellent example of the kingdom of God is the parable of the sower found in Matthew 13. In this chapter, Jesus talked about the mysteries of the kingdom of heaven which were given to His disciples, but rejected by the Jewish religious leaders in their rejection of Him (see chapter twelve). Matthew also included a digression (13:10-23) in which Jesus explained to His disciples why He spoke in parables and interpreted the parable of the sower. D. A Carson notes that, "These digressions would have taken place after the public discourse (suggested by the use of the plural "parables"), and that Matthew includes them as parentheses so that the significance of the parables will not be lost to the reader."[50]

In the parable of the sower, Jesus referred to "the kingdom of heaven" rather than the kingdom of God." Thomas Ramsdell notes, "It is well known that the spirit of reverence among the Jews was so great that they systematically avoided the pronunciation of the divine name. Hence, Matthew, writing principally for Jews, respects this feeling, and speaks of the Kingdom of Heaven instead of the Kingdom of God."[51] In Matthew, the word "parable" does not occur until chapter thirteen. Jack Dean Kingsley wrote,

The parables in Matthew 13 were given in some measure as an apology against the Jews for their rejection of Christ . . . This chapter is a great turning point in Matthew's presentation. Jesus was preaching and teaching the kingdom to the Jews, but they rejected Him. In reaction to this rejection Jesus

---

[50] D. A. Carson, *Matthew: Expositor's Bible Commentary* (Grand Rapids: Zondervan, 1984), 46.
[51] Thomas J Ramsdell, *"The Kingdom of Heaven in the Gospel,"* The Biblical World Vol. 4, No. 2 Chicago: The University of Chicago Press, (August, 1894):124. Internet available at: https://www.jstor.org/stable/3135427?seq=1#metadata_info_tab_contents

presented the parables to show them they were no longer the privileged people to whom God would impart His revelation, but instead they were in danger of being judged by the Son of Man for having spurned their Messiah.[52]

John P. Maier observed, "The very fact that Jesus now withdraws into a parabolic form of teaching is a sign of judgment upon Israel."[53]

Jesus said that the secrets of the kingdom of heaven were given to the disciples, but not to others. The kingdom realities described in Matthew's parables are different from the splendor of the Davidic kingdom described in the Old Testament. Jesus did not bring the kingdom in with a bang as described in the Old Testament, but quietly brought it in through the hearts of people. The mysteries of the kingdom are revealed to those who accept Jesus. The kingdom of God is here, but God does not force it upon humankind. People can either accept it or reject it. If they are looking for an earthly king who will come and solve all of their problems, they will miss it. Showing how the mysteries of the kingdom differed from the Old Testament expectations, Ladd wrote: "That there should be a coming of God's kingdom in the way Jesus proclaimed, in a hidden secret form, working quietly among men, was utterly

[52] Jack Dean Kingsbury, *Matthew 13: A Study of Redaction Criticism* (Richmond: John Knox Press, 1969), 31.
[53] John P. Maier, *The Vision of Matthew: Christ, Church, and Morality in the First Gospel* (New York: Paulist Press, 1978), 90.

novel to Jesus' contemporaries. The Old Testament gave no such promises."[54] Disciples have been born into the kingdom of darkness, but it was never intended to be a permanent home. Many who have not accepted Jesus as Savior are not experiencing the beautiful richness of the joy, peace, and freedom of God's kingdom. "The Kingdom of God has come into the world to be received by some but rejected by others. The Kingdom is in the present to have only partial success, and this success is dependent upon a human response."[55] J. Dwight Pentecost wrote, "But what the Old Testament had not revealed was that an entire age would intervene between the offer of the kingdom by the Messiah and Israel's reception of the King and enjoyment of full kingdom blessings."[56]

Matthew 13 opens with Jesus leaving the house and sitting down by the sea. A great multitude gathered around Him, so He got into a boat and sat down. The multitudes sat on the shore. These details provide the setting for all the parables in Matthew 13. Jesus began the parable by introducing the characters of the sower, the seed, the birds, the sun, and the thorns. In the story, the seed is the main character; all the other characters are performing an action with the seed. These characters are described by Mark Allan Powell as "'stock characters,'

---

[54] Ladd, *The Presence of the Future*, 225.
[55] Ibid., 230.
[56] J. Dwight Pentecost, *Thy Kingdom Come* (Wheaton: Victor, 1990), 219.

those with a single trait who perform a perfunctory role in the story."[57]

Before Matthew recorded Jesus's words, he said that Jesus told them many things in parables (Matthew 13:3). Parables are simple stories used to illustrate a moral or spiritual lesson, as told by Jesus in the Gospels. John R. Donahue wrote, "Parables are communications that take place through the use of images rather than literal or precise speech."[58] In this particular parable Jesus said in verse 3 that a sower went out into his field to sow seed manually. As he sowed the seeds, some of it fell in various areas both in and around the field. In this parable, Jesus was offering an earthly picture of what it means to respond to the Word of God. There are three main elements of this parable.

The first main element of this parable is the seed. The seed represents the Word of God, or the "Word of the kingdom," which is more than just the Bible. The seed is the Word of the kingdom as it is preached, the proclamation of the truth of the gospel of Jesus Christ, the good news of salvation and eternal life, the spiritual food needed to live life in light of God's kingdom. The psalmist said, "Your word *is* a lamp to my feet And a light to my path" (Psalm 119:105).

---

[57] Mark Allan Powell, *What is Narrative Criticism* (Minneapolis: Fortress Press, 1990), 55.
[58] John R Donahue, *The Gospel in Parables* (Minneapolis: Fortress Press, 1990), 6.

The second main element of this parable is the sower. The sower in this parable represents Christ, who scattered the seed Himself and now uses believers to do the same. In Romans 10:14, Paul asked a series of rhetorical questions: "How then shall they call on Him in whom they have not believed? And how shall they believe in Him of whom they have not heard? And how shall they hear without a preacher?" In this parable, Christ is the sower, who continues to sow the seed of the Word through His followers.

The third main element of this parable is the soil. The soil represents the hearts of those who hear the Word through preaching. There are many who hear the Word of God, but respond very differently. Every kind of soil represents a different kind of hearer. The truth is being proclaimed, but the question is, "How does one respond to the true preaching of the gospel?" In this parable, Jesus identified four kinds of soil.

First, in verse 4, Jesus said, "Some seeds fell by the wayside." The seed was sown, but the birds came and devoured it. In verse 19, Jesus explained: "When anyone hears the word of the kingdom, and does not understand it, then the wicked one comes and snatches away what was sown in his heart. Commenting on the same parable as given in Luke 8:4-15, J. Vernon McGee notes, "The birds are the symbol of the Devil."[59] There

---

[59] J. Vernon McGee, *Thru the Bible Commentary, volume 4* (Nashville: Thomas Nelson Publishers, 1983), 74.

are several things to note in this verse. First, Jesus said this person did not understand what he or she heard. Second, He said that "the wicked one" (Satan) snatches it away from his or her heart. The heart of each person who hears the gospel is compared to the soil receiving the farmer's seed. In this case, the heart is as hard as a roadside. So, when the gospel is preached, Satan snatches away the word, like birds quickly eating seed that falls on the hard ground of a roadside. Ladd notes, "Some hear the word of the Kingdom but it never enters their heart. They hear the Gospel of the Kingdom but they do not understand the truth which they hear. Satan comes and snatches away the seed. There is no root, there is no life."[60] This is a picture of those who come to church service Sunday after Sunday. They hear the gospel, but it is snatched away from their hearts "immediately" by Satan. It can also describe those who have been coming to church for a long time, but still remain unconverted. The soil by the roadside represents that kind of person's heart. The soil receives the seed, but the soil has not been prepared to the point where the seed penetrates the soil. The seed does not grow to produce any fruit in this type of soil. This is a heart that is stubborn and rebellious against God's Word that actively rejects the Word of God. This is a heart that would criticize rather that embrace the preached Word.

---

[60] George Eldon Ladd, *The Presence of the Kingdom* (Grand Rapids: Eerdmans, 1974), 137.

Second, in verses 5 and 6, Jesus said that "some seed fell on stony ground." This is the ground which is just a thin layer of soil over rock, which, according to Jesus, represents the one who "hears the word and immediately receives it with joy; yet he has no root in himself, but endures only for a while" (verses 20-21). For when tribulation or persecution arises because of the word, immediately he stumbles." This kind of soil represents someone who is excited and happy about hearing the Word. In fact, this person may actually praise preaching, which is where the trouble begins. He or she may receive it "with joy" (Matthew 13:20), but the seed does not take root. There is no conviction of sin or sorrow for sin. This kind of soil represents an emotional "decision for Christ," not a genuine work of conversion. Therefore, when trouble comes, this person falls away because he or she was never converted in the first place. This kind of soil represents people who might appear to produce fruit because of their zeal, but soon the excitement dies for lack of root. They are excited, but the Word does not go deep enough to bear any fruit. And because there is no depth, just as soon as persecution arises because of the Word, they are offended. McGee notes, "The "rocky places" are those who receive the Word of God in the enthusiasm of the flesh. Trouble and persecution dampen the interest. For a time, fleshly hearers of the Word manifest great interest and zeal, but a little trouble reveals their lack of true faith."[61] The persecution that the text mentions is something that is inevitable for the people of God. Literally the word *persecution* means "to be pressed in on every side." Paul said, "*We are* hard-pressed on every side, yet not crushed; *we are* perplexed, but not in despair; persecuted, but not forsaken; struck down, but not destroyed" (2 Corinthians 4:9). It is as though disciples are pressed into a corner. They are pursued. They are hunted down by the ungodly.

Third, in verse 7, Jesus said, "And some fell among thorns and the thorns sprung up and choked them." This type of soil has weeds in it. The weeds take away all the nutrients from the good seed. The result is that the seed cannot grow and produce any fruit. In verse 22, Jesus explained: "Now he who received seed among the thorns is he who hears the word, and the cares of this world and the deceitfulness of riches choke the word, and he becomes unfruitful." This kind of soil represents a hearer who is preoccupied with the cares of this world and does not even hear the Word. Jesus explained that the weeds represent the cares of the world that preoccupy people, cause them to worry, and distract them from hearing God's Word. David Wenham wrote, "Sometimes there is response, but then the word is gradually strangled by competing forces, 'the cares of the world, the deceit of wealth and desires

---

[61] McGee, 74.

for other things.'"[62] Many people have been deceived into thinking that the more riches they have, the happier they will be. They are persuaded by that big lie of Satan because they lack the power of the Word of God. Munroe notes, "The kingdom of darkness gets its power from that which we do not know. The truth we are ignorant of cannot protect us against Satan's deception. That is why we must devote ourselves to studying, learning, experiencing and practicing the Word of God. The light of knowledge dispels the darkness of deception and ignorance; the light of truth destroys the darkness of lies and error."[63]

Fourth, in verse 8, Jesus said, "But others fell on good ground and brought forth fruit: some a hundredfold, some sixty, some thirty." This kind of soil represents a person whose heart is softened and ready to be receptive to the Word of God. David Wenham wrote, "Those on the good soil are those who listen to the message, receive it, and in due course bear fruit, living out in practice the life of the revolution".[64] People who are receptive know they need the Word of God to engage in a spiritual battle on earth. They need spiritual nourishment for their souls. They know they are sinners, but they need to hear that Christ has forgiven them. They need to hear about God's grace to them, because they are remorseful about their sins.

---

[62] David Wenham, *The Parables of Jesus* (Downers Grove: InterVarsity Press, 1989), 47.
[63] Munroe, 88.
[64] Wenham, 47.

They need the grace of Christ to strengthen their faith. These hearers want to hear the Word of God, and become stronger in their faith. They realize how empty life would be without the Word of God. It would be very difficult for them to survive without it. They are hungry for the Word of God. They bear much fruit because the soil is fertile. They hear and obey the Word of God, which produces the fruit of the Spirit as found in Galatians: "But the fruit of the Spirit is love, joy, peace, longsuffering, kindness, goodness, faithfulness, gentleness, self-control. Against such there is no law" (Galatians 5:22-23). Jesus said that these hearers will bear fruit, "some a hundredfold, some sixty, some thirty." Matthew Henry wrote, "Among fruitful Christians, some are more fruitful than others: where there is true grace, yet there are degrees of it; some of greater attainments in knowledge and holiness than others; all Christ's scholars are not in the same form."[65] In Mark's version of this parable, Jesus said that the crops "grew up and increased" (4:8). Mark wrote of an ascending order of "thirty, sixty, and a hundredfold" (4:8, 20). Matthew spoke of a descending order of "a hundredfold, some sixty, and some thirty" (13:8, 23), whereas Luke mentioned the singular expression, "a crop a hundred times as great" (8:8). Alan Hugh McNeile wrote that "Mark's order is the natural one, and that Matthew's is reversed to "indicate more clearly that even in the

---

[65] Henry, 151.

fruit-bearing hearers of the word there are gradations."[66] War-ren W. Wiersbe sums up Jesus's teaching in this way, "It is important to note that none of these first three hearts underwent salvation. The proof of salvation is not listening to the Word, or having a quick emotional response to the Word, or even cultivating the Word . . . the proof of salvation is *fruit*, for as Christ said, 'Ye shall know them by their fruits.'"[67]

Jesus ended the parable in verse 9 by saying, "He who has ears to hear, let him hear!" This phrase is mentioned many times throughout the Bible. Jesus is not talking about hearing audibly, but about hearing in terms of conformity (obedience). This point is also made profoundly in the letter of James:

But be doers of the word, and not hearers only, deceiving yourselves. For if anyone is a hearer of the word and not a doer, he is like a man observing his natural face in a mirror; for he observes himself, goes away, and immediately forgets what kind of man he was. But he who looks into the perfect law of liberty and continues *in it*, and is not a forgetful hearer but a doer of the work, this one will be blessed in what he does" (James 1:22-25).

---

[66] Alan Hugh McNeile, *The Gospel according to Matthew* (Grand Rapids: Baker, 1980), 185.
[67] Warren W. Wiersbe, *Meet Yourself in the Parables* (Wheaton: Victor Books, 1979), 27.

To be a disciple is not only to hear the word (i.e., get that initial look into the mirror), but also to adjust to the Word.

When Jesus finished this parable, the disciples asked Him in verse 10, "Why do You speak to them in parables?" Jesus's answer in verse 12 was profound:

"Whoever has will be given more, and they will have an abundance. Whoever does not have, even what they have will be taken from them." He spoke in parables to conceal truth from those who reject and to reveal truth to those who accept. Jesus was speaking about accepting the truth and acting upon that truth. If disciples respond to truth, more truth will be given to them. If they reject the truth, they shall have the truth taken from them. The point is that if disciples believe this parable and act on it by faith and obedience, they will be given more truth. But those who reject these truths shall have them taken away. "He who has ears, let him hear!" J. Vernon McGee wrote, "The Lord will never shut the door to one who wants to hear. He makes it clear that this is His reason for speaking in parables. Those who don't want to hear will not understand them."[68]

The parable of the sower is very relevant to the twenty-first century church. All four of these soils are represented in the

---

[68] McGee, 74.

church. The ultimate purpose of disciples is to bear fruit for the kingdom of God. The key Scripture that helps disciples stay on track is Matthew 6:33: "But seek first the kingdom of God and His righteousness, and all these things shall be added to you." The Word says in Matthew 7:16, "By their fruit you shall know them." Disciples walk as sanctified believers of God's kingdom. The Word of the kingdom has given them new life and they walk in the fullness of it with thankfulness to God. Disciples need to examine themselves daily to ensure God is truly the most important Person in their lives. Those who seek truth and knowledge will grow in their maturity, while those who reject will remain in ignorance. Jack Dean Kingsbury wrote, "We have the choice to either respond to the story with a desire to understand or to reject its message as having little impact or meaning in our lives. Whether two thousand years ago or today, their intended purpose is the same: to bring the life of the recipient into conformity with Jesus."[69]

Regarding new converts, W. D. Davies and Dale C. Allison wrote, "When people do become Christians, we should not expect them all to bear fruit immediately. Hearing comes first, then understanding, then fruit-bearing naturally follows."[70] We should not expect that every believer will bear fruit at the same pace. Every person is different and some will grow faster

---

[69] Jack Dean Kingsbury, *Matthew As Story* (Philadelphia: Fortress Press, 1988), 110.
[70] W. D. Davies and Dale C. Allison, Jr. *Matthew 8-18: International Critical Commentary* (New York: Bloomsbury T&T Clark, 1991), 374.

than others. As Davies and Allison further note, "Opportunity does not guarantee response, proclamation does not abolish sin."[71]

In the twenty-first century, disciples of Jesus Christ must continue to learn, teach and preach the good news of the kingdom of God. It will not be enough for a disciple only to hear the word, but they must live out the word in their daily lives. Disciples of Jesus Christ have been brought out of darkness into the kingdom of God's marvelous light. In Colossians 1:13-14, Paul said, "For He delivered us from the power of darkness, and conveyed us into the kingdom of Son of His love, in whom we have redemption through His blood, the forgiveness of sins." And in Romans 14:17, he wrote, "For the kingdom of God is not eating and drinking, but righteousness and peace and joy in the Holy Spirit" (Romans 14:17). Chapter four will present a survey of discipleship in the book of Acts, and will show how the process of discipleship that Jesus used with the first disciples will transform a church and a culture.

---

[71] Ibid., 403.

SURVEY OF DISCIPLESHIP IN THE BOOK OF ACTS

Chapter three surveys the book of Acts and the great devotion of the disciples to Jesus. The authorship of the book of Acts is attributed to Luke, who was an educated Greek physician (Colossians 4:14). In the first century, the disciples within the church were the eye-witnesses to the life and ministry of Jesus Christ. These eye-witnesses followed the process of discipleship that Jesus used in making them to be His followers. This process, if followed, will transform a church and culture. The first disciples led the early church through the formation of the Word of God, the transformation of the Word, and the application of the Word.

They led the church toward spiritual maturity. They were fed by Jesus for three years as they walked with Him; but after His death and resurrection, they received the great commission, which is found in Matthew 28:18-20. They went throughout the entire known world of their day sharing the good news of the kingdom of God. The book of Acts gives a historical account of the church's beginnings. It describes the birth of the church at Pentecost, and the power of the Holy Spirit in the lives of believers. An excellent example of the power of the Holy Spirit is when Peter and John healed the lame man at the gate of the temple called Beautiful. Peter was so empowered by the Holy Spirit that he made a profound statement in Acts 3:6: "Silver and gold I do not have, but what I do have I give you: In the name of Jesus Christ of Nazareth, rise up and walk." The book of Acts offers principles for living in the midst of persecutions and hardships. It serves as a reminder that the gospel is available for everyone, Jews and Gentiles alike. It brings deliverance and freedom to all who call upon the name of Jesus and gives people the hope that they can be saved. Another focus in the book of Acts is the conversion of Saul, and the great testimony he had as a result of his conversion.

The book of Acts is also a guide for the church today. Many church growth principles are found in this book. These principles that show how the gospel spread from Jerusalem to Rome are still practical in the twenty-first century. The book of Acts demonstrates that God's hand is in everything and that church growth was not just the work of people, but also the work of God. It is a guide for the church in choosing godly leaders, and a witness to the power of prayer. For example, in Acts 16 when Paul and Silas were in the Philippian jail, they were praying and singing hymns to God before the earthquake shook the very foundation of the prison. This book also displays the power of a personal testimony and gives a clear demonstration of what Christian discipleship looks like. The major theme in the book of Acts is that Jesus came to advance His kingdom. His mission was to see His kingdom spread throughout the world drawing men and women to Himself through His life, death, and resurrection. What Jesus did and taught during His earthly ministry, He is continuing to do from heaven. Acts is a story about men and women having an encounter with the resurrected Jesus, who is very much alive and reigning in heaven. It was Jesus who saved the souls of people as they heard the Word. It was Jesus who converted the unbelieving Saul, who became one of the greatest missionaries the world has ever seen. It is Jesus who still establishes and gives directions to church leaders, missionaries, and church planters. In other words, Jesus is still advancing the kingdom of God through the power of the Holy Spirit.

Chapter one of the book of Acts gives the twenty-first century disciple a display of the power of the Holy Spirit. Just before Jesus's ascension, He gathered His disciples and commanded them not to leave Jerusalem, but to wait for the promise of the Father, "which," He said, "you have heard from Me; **for John truly baptized with water, but you shall be baptized with the Holy Spirit not many days from now"** (Acts 1:4-5). This promise was fulfilled in an extraordinary at the birth of the church in Acts chapter two. When Jesus's promise of the Spirit's coming was fulfilled, something supernatural from heaven occurred. The book of Acts is about what the local church looks like when the Holy Spirit takes over.

What did Jesus's promise really mean? The disciples had spent more than three years listening to Jesus teach and watching Him work. They had spent three-plus years absorbing truth from the eternal Son of God, who was preparing them to be foundation stones in the church. The disciples were not lacking in information to do what God wanted them to do, but Jesus knew they were lacking in power. And even though He had been their Bible teacher, He told them that they wouldn't have power until the Holy Spirit came. The disciples asked Jesus, "Lord, will You at this time restore the kingdom of Israel" (Acts 1:6). Dickson notes, "The disciples no doubt believed Jesus was the Messiah, but in line with general Jewish thinking they hoped Jesus the Messiah must establish

Israel as supreme on earth."[72] Jesus answered, "It is not for you to know times or seasons which the Father has put in His own authority. But **you shall receive power when the Holy Spirit has come upon you;** and you shall be witnesses to Me in Jerusalem, and in all Judea and Samaria, and to the end of the earth" (Acts 1:6-8). J. Vernon McGee said, "This is the commission that still holds for today. This is not given only to a corporate body, to the church as a body; it is not a corporate commission. This is a very personal command to each believer— personally, privately."[73] After the resurrection, Jesus told His disciples to wait in Jerusalem until they were bestowed with *power* from on high, power to be his witnesses unto the ends of the earth. When the feast of Pentecost had fully come, the church was born and God poured out His Holy Spirit in Jerusalem. The ultimate goal of the Holy Spirit's coming to indwell believers at Pentecost is the building of God's kingdom. In essence, Jesus was also saying, "No Spirit equals no power." The Spirit is the third Person of the Godhead, of one substance with the Father, fully God, coequal to and co-eternal with the Father and Son.

Many people have a hold on God the Father, and they know that He is their Creator. And many people have no problem with God the Son. They know that Jesus is their Savior. But

---

[72] Kwesi A. Dickson, *The Story of the Early Church* (London: Darton, Longman, &Todd Ltd, 1976), 20.
[73] McGee, 512.

for many people, the concept of the Holy Spirit is a little fuzzy, a little vague. What or who was it that Jesus was promising? Throughout the Gospels and into the book of Acts Jesus promised the disciples that they would not be left alone. The Holy Spirit was not a last-minute thought by Christ. Before Jesus began His earthly ministry, He was announced by his cousin John the Baptist who said in Matthew 3:11, "I indeed baptize you with water unto repentance, but He who is coming after me is mightier than I, whose sandals I am not worthy to carry. He will baptize you with the Holy Spirit and fire." And so it should have come as no surprise when hours before His arrest Jesus told His disciples in John 14:16-17, "And I will pray the Father, and He will give you another Helper, that He may abide with you forever—the Spirit of truth, whom the world cannot receive, because it neither sees Him nor knows Him; but you know Him, for He dwells with you and will be in you." It was Jesus Himself who alerted them to the absolutely critical role that the Holy Spirit was to play in the church, and it was Jesus who promised to send the Spirit after His ascension back to the Father. On the night before His crucifixion, Jesus told the disciples in John 16:7, "I tell you the truth, it is to your advantage that I go away, for if I do not go away, the Helper will not come to you, but if I go, I will send Him to you." Many believers would rather Jesus be here today than have the Holy Spirit. But believers are better off with the

Spirit's presence than with the presence of the historical Jesus. Jesus limited Himself in the flesh, but the Spirit pervades and invades every place and permanently indwells every believer (John 14:17b) because He is the omnipresent God, the third Person of the Trinity.

The Holy Spirit is a Person. He is our comforter, counselor, guide, and teacher. More importantly, He is God.

The Holy Spirit is a Person. He is our comforter, counselor, guide, and teacher. More importantly, He is God. The Holy Spirit has always existed because he is God. The Holy Spirit existed at creation when God said, "Let Us make man in Our image" (Genesis 1:26). The Holy Spirit is not an option in the disciple's life. The Holy Spirit is the power of a disciple's Christian experience. The Holy Spirit is at the very center of a disciple's life and helps him or her live an obedient, productive, fruitful Christian life. A transliteration of the Greek word for Holy Spirit is *Paraclete*, which means advocate, intercessor, consoler, comforter, or who comes along to help the disciple. Jesus assured His disciples that even though He would leave, they would not be left alone. There would be another divine Person who would take His place in their midst. This person would be with them as Jesus had been with them for comfort, strength, and guidance, but this Person would also be in them. Jesus wanted the disciples to know He was going to send them a somebody, not a something. Evans said, "One of the fundamental problems is that we look for the wrong thing first when it comes to the Holy Ghost. People talk about their need for Holy Ghost power. Now make no mistake about it, we do need Holy Ghost power. But only after we have met Holy Ghost *Person*."[74]

In this twenty-first century, disciples of Jesus Christ must ensure that they are not just focused on the power and miss the relationship with the Person. The Holy Spirit is a knowable and relatable Person, not just a force or power to be used. The disciple must have the Person of the Holy Spirit and the power of the Holy Spirit to carry out the work of the kingdom of God effectively.

A great example of the Holy Spirit's power was the birth of the church on the day of Pentecost in chapter two. On the day of Pentecost, the disciples were baptized in the Holy Spirit. Pentecost was the church's birthday, and it was the power and activity of the Holy Spirit that brought the church into being. Pentecost means "fiftieth day." It corresponds to the Jewish Feast of Weeks, which was a one-day religious observance that

---

[74] Tony Evans, *The Promise* (Chicago: Moody Press, 1996), 18.

came fifty days after Passover. Pentecost comes fifty days after Passover day. Passover is the anniversary of the deliverance of the Hebrew people from Egyptian slavery, and the Feast of Weeks is the anniversary of God's constitution for the establishment of a new nation. Without the law, the state of Israel in the Promised Land could never have come into existence. Likewise, Easter, as the anniversary of the resurrection, is the celebration of Christ's conquest of death and His victory over the grave. Matthew Henry notes:

> The Holy Ghost came down at the time of a solemn feast, because there was then a concourse of people to Jerusalem from all parts of the country, and the proselytes from other countries, which would make it the more public, and the fame of it to be spread the sooner and further, which would contribute much to the propagating of the gospel into all nations.[75]

William Cannon states, "Pentecost signalizes the gift of the power of the resurrection to Christ's followers and the constitution of the new Israel—the church—to supersede the old Israel."[76] From a human standpoint, two factors contributed to the quick and widespread effects of the Holy Spirit's power

---

[75] Henry, 11.
[76] William R. Cannon, *The Book of Acts* (Nashville: Upper Room Books, 1989), 27.

on the day of Pentecost. The first factor was that the first disciples of this emerging church were of "one accord." They were of a single mind. The second factor was that the people were gathered together in one place. They were not scattered abroad. When this event took place, they all participated in it. The church was born through people who were assembled together in one place. With these two factors in place, the Holy Spirit came and transformed that small assembly of people into the first congregation of the Christian church. Luke uses two symbols—wind and fire—to describe the descent of the Holy Spirit. The Spirit's presence was manifested as wind and fire, a powerful invasion from heaven that the disciples had never known before.

Luke says that those present heard a sound out of heaven like a mighty rushing wind blowing through the whole house. Then, what looked like flames or tongues of fire appeared and settled on each of them, and all that were present were filled with the Holy Spirit and began speaking in other languages, as the Holy Spirit gave them this ability. The Holy Spirit was manifested to them by what they heard and what they saw. The blowing, whistling wind illustrates the pervasiveness of the Holy Spirit, which reached and affected everyone in that first Christian congregation. Fire illustrates the guidance the Holy Spirit would give the followers of Jesus as they undertook their mission in the world. The Spirit would show them what to do and how to do it. He would enable them to convict people of sin, warn them about God's judgment, and make them righteous (John 16:8). In other words, what the Spirit did for them at Pentecost, He would do through the church for all those who believe and accept the gospel message. At Pentecost those people were set on fire spiritually by the Holy Spirit. They gained divine energy; they no longer operated as mere human beings. Their strength and influence were the strength and energy of almighty God. When Luke said that they were all filled with the Holy Spirit, he meant that they were controlled or saturated by the Spirit. In Galatians 5:18, Paul wrote "And be not drunk with wine, wherein is excess; but be filled with the Spirit." They no longer belonged to themselves, but to God. It was no longer they who lived but Christ by the Holy Spirit who lived in them (Galatians 2:20).

And there were dwelling in Jerusalem Jews, devout men from every nation under heaven. And when this sound occurred, the multitude came together, and were confused, because everyone heard them speak in his own language. They were amazed and marveled, saying to one another "Look, are not all these who speak Galileans? And how is it that we hear, each in own language in in which we were born?" (Acts 2:6-8). We hear them telling in our own language the mighty works of God. Luke said, "So they were amazed and perplexed, saying to one another, "Whatever could this mean?" Others mocking said, "They are full of new wine" (Acts 2:12-13).

Cannon notes, "The languages were not unknown tongues in the sense of being something different from any languages spoken by people on earth. What each spoke was unknown to them before they spoke it, but it was not unknown to those to whom it was spoken."[77] When the Holy Spirit came with power, the disciples were able to speak in a way they had never been able to speak before, declaring the message of God in a number of languages they had not previously learned. The purpose of speaking in other tongues was not for the personal edification of the disciples, but simply as a means of converting unbelievers. Everyone who was there was amazed and perplexed to hear the presumably ignorant Galileans conversing fluently with people in different languages.

In chapter two, the very first act of this newly constituted Christian congregation was to preach the gospel to unbelievers. Evangelizing is the soul of Christianity. Reiner states, "In the churches in Acts, we see an evangelistic zeal and endeavor to bring the community outside the church to salvation in Jesus Christ. We cannot help but discern that evangelism was the church's highest priority. Because evangelism was the final command issued by the risen Lord, it became the very source

---

[77] Ibid., 29.

of life for the churches in Acts."[78] After the Spirit descended on the church at Pentecost, its members did not remain in the upper room to sing hymns together, pray for one another, and reenact Jesus' last meal with them by breaking and eating bread and drinking wine together in memory of His death, burial and resurrection. They went immediately into the streets of Jerusalem to witness to others and to announce the good news about Jesus Christ.

In the twenty-first century, disciples of Jesus Christ must come out of the four walls of the church and into the communities to witness to the lost and spread the good news of Jesus Christ.

In the twenty-first century, disciples of Jesus Christ must come out of the four walls of the church and into the communities to witness to the lost and spread the good news of Jesus Christ. The church was not called to be a maintenance church just to satisfy its members, but to go out to the highways and byways to reach the lost for the kingdom of God.

The first sermon to be preached was delivered by Peter in Jerusalem on the day of Pentecost. The first ministers were

---

[78] Thom S. Rainer, *"Church Growth and Evangelism in the Book of Acts,"* Criswell Theological Review 5.1 (1990) 68. Internet available at: Church Growth and Evangelism in the Book of Acts (gordon.edu)

the disciples, and their primary responsibility was to preach the gospel. Peter used the accusation of the mockers in the crowd that the disciples were drunk as the lead-in to his sermon. He said, "For these are not drunk, as you suppose, since it is only the third hour of the day" (Acts 2:15). In essence, they would not be drunk at nine o'clock in the morning. What the crowd saw in those witnesses was a demonstration of the power of the Holy Spirit prophesied by Joel in the Old Testament (Joel 2:28-32). The disciples of Jesus, inspired by the Holy Spirit, had dreamed dreams and seen visions, and they could not help prophesying. Earlier, God had shown miracles, wonders, and signs on the earth through Jesus of Nazareth. Peter noted that this Jesus, whom the Jews had crucified had been raised and was sitting at the right hand of the Father. This Jesus, who had demonstrated that God approved Him by miracles and wonders, had been arrested and convicted by the very people to whom Peter preached. They were the ones who caused Him to be crucified by the Romans. Peter denounced them for this in his sermon, accusing them of killing their own Messiah. But God raised Jesus from the dead, as King David prophesied. Peter interpreted David's word in Psalm 16: 8-11 as a description of what would happen to the Messiah. He told the crowd that David could not have been describing himself, for David had died and his tomb was visible to them in Jerusalem.

Jesus of Nazareth was the Person whose soul God would not leave among the dead. It was He whom God raised up to sit at God's right hand in glory. It was Jesus the Messiah who had sent the Holy Spirit to empower Peter and the other disciples, and the people were witnessing in them the demonstrations of the Spirit. The people at large had not witnessed the resurrection. Only the disciples and followers of Jesus had seen the empty tomb immediately after Jesus's resurrection, and had fellowship with Him after His resurrection. And they alone had watched Him ascend to heaven. But the demonstrations of the Holy Spirit in words and deeds of the disciples and the other followers of Jesus on the day of Pentecost were public acts that anyone who was present could have seen and heard. Peter brought his powerful sermon to a close by proclaiming that God had made this Jesus whom the house of Israel crucified both Lord and Christ.

The people were deeply moved by Peter's sermon. He convinced them of the truth of what he said and convicted them of their sins. Their response to the message was immediate and positive. They asked Peter and the other apostles what they should do. They wanted to be told how to change their lives and become acceptable to God. They wanted to know how they could be saved. Then Peter said to them, "Repent, and let every one of you be baptized in the name of Jesus Christ for the remission of sins; and you shall receive the gift of the

Holy Spirit" (Acts 2:38). Then they would receive a double gift: the forgiveness of their sins and the gift of the Holy Spirit. In other words, the new disciples could expect the same empowerment by the Holy Spirit, which they had witnessed in the words and deeds of the apostles who had known and loved the Lord when He sojourned with them on earth. The gifts of the Spirit might differ in each of the believers, but like the disciples, each believer would become an effective witness of Jesus Christ. One more observation about Peter's sermon is that Peter mentioned a promise: "For the promise is to you and to your children, and to all who are afar off, as many as the Lord our God will call" (Acts 2:39). The offer would first be made to the nation of Israel, then to Samaria, and ultimately to the uttermost part of the earth. M.R DeHaan notes, "If the nation of Israel had received this second offer of the Kingdom, their Messiah would have returned; but God knew this offer would also be rejected, and so planned His program for the Church after the Gospel had been given *to the Jew first*, and rejected by them."[79]

As a result of Peter's sermon on the day of Pentecost, three thousand people were converted in one day. And as they took their places as new members of the emerging church, they continued in an unwavering way in the apostles' doctrine and fellowship. The believing church community gradually began

---

[79] M. R. DeHaan, *Pentecost and After* (Grand Rapids: Zondervan Publishing House, 1964), 49.

to take shape. Many of the characteristics of the early church still exist in the twenty-first century church today. At its heart was the teaching ministry of the apostles who had been with Jesus, listened to His words, and knew His mind. The apostles began to teach and preach the truth of the Word of God to nurture and edify the body of Christ. The church was a place of fellowship where members shared common meals among themselves. As worshipers, they ate bread and drank wine ceremoniously in remembrance of their Lord's death and in anticipation of His coming. They also shared what they had with one another, putting their material resources at the disposal of the congregation as needs arose. They still worshiped daily in the temple, but they also met in one another's homes that they might increase in their understanding of the apostles' doctrine. As they praised God and as the apostles did many wonders and signs, they found favor with all the people, and every day new disciples were added to the church. What were the results of the day of Pentecost and the benefits for the twenty-first century church today?

First, Pentecost reveals the work of the triune God in our salvation. Just as creation was the work of the Trinity, the day of Pentecost was also a demonstration of the Godhead's redemptive work. The Father is the source of all redemptive acts of God. The Son is the representative of the mission of God. The work of salvation is accomplished through His birth, life, death and resurrection. The Holy Spirit is the empowering presence of God who makes us holy through sanctification. Since the day of Pentecost, the church as the people of God has been indwelled and energized by the Holy Spirit. The Holy Spirit is God Himself acting in this world and in our lives. He draws us by His grace to the Father. He intercedes with us and within us, helping us to pray. The Holy Spirit teaches and admonishes disciples when they read and study the Word. The Spirit is the disciple's divine Teacher. During Jesus's conversation with His disciples in the upper room before the crucifixion, He referred to the Spirit's future teaching ministry. Jesus said, "But the Helper, the Holy Spirit, whom the Father will send in My name, He will teach you all things, and bring to your remembrance all things that I said to you" (John 14:26). The Spirit's job is to take the Word of God and bring it alive in the lives of believers. He gives believers the gift of discernment so that they might have the mind of Christ and think about things in ways that are informed by godly wisdom. He applies and nurtures the fruit of the Spirit in the lives of believers (love, joy, peace, patience, goodness, kindness, gentleness, faithfulness, and self-control). The Holy Spirit assures us of our forgiveness and our adoption as the children of God. In short, the Holy Spirit mediates the presence of God in our lives and in the church.

Second, The Holy Spirit empowers the church for effective service, witness, and global mission. The Holy Spirit is the power of the church, in the same way that the engine in a car supplies the power to make the car go. Without this power source the church may look good, like a new car sitting in the parking lot, but will not be going anywhere. That is because living the Christian life without the active participation of the Holy Spirit is impossible. It is possible to know the Bible and not know the Lord; to memorize Bible verses, to come to church every Sunday, and yet not be transformed, because only the Holy Spirit can make what is true in the Bible become real in a disciple's life. It is impossible for believers to be the disciples God intended them to be apart from the dynamic ministry of the Holy Spirit. Jesus said, "Apart from Me you can do nothing" (John 15:5). Apart from Jesus, believers can do nothing that glorifies Him, because Jesus is the One who sent the Holy Spirit to indwell and empower the disciple and the church. Jesus promised that the Holy Spirit would empower disciples to be His witnesses to the ends of the earth (Acts 1:8). It is the Holy Spirit who enables the church to serve sacrificially and to be an effective witness for Christ and the gospel. Holiness is not just about making people personally righteous, but it is also about extending God's glory and righteousness to all the people of this world! There is a harvest of people out there who still have not received the good news about Jesus Christ.

It is the Holy Spirit who ensures that the gospel is proclaimed to the ends of the earth through the empowered witness of the church. The disciples were able to do things they had never done before because they were filled with the Holy Spirit. What is missing in the church today is not programs and seminars and information. The church is missing the Holy Spirit's power that comes from His filling. The more Spirit-filled Christians the church has, the fewer programs it needs. The church's job is not to replace the Spirit's ministry with other things, even good things. Having everything in place and being organized is fine, but the church has to make sure that members do not organize themselves out of the need for the Holy Spirit.

Third, The Holy Spirit reveals the signs and wonders of the kingdom of God. The Holy Spirit is the One who continues to manifest redemptive signs of God's kingdom breaking into the world. The good news of God's powerful work in this world did not stop at the cross and the resurrection of Jesus Christ. Disciples are called not simply to proclaim something that happened in history thousands of years ago, but to proclaim the resurrected power of Christ today to transform lives. All the future expectations of the promise of eternal life are breaking into the world now through the presence of the Holy Spirit. Men and women are healed by the power of the Holy Spirit. Disciples can experience forgiveness and reconciliation with one another. The poor and downcast can receive hope. The Holy Spirit helps disciples to be new creations in Jesus Christ. This process will not be fully complete until Jesus returns; but until that time a disciple can see that God is still at work by His Spirit, reconciling the world to Himself.

Fourth, The Holy Spirit is the One who makes believers holy. The presence of the Holy Spirit, God's empowering presence in the lives of believers, leads to transformational holiness in the lives of believers, in society, in the church and in the world. The holiness of God demands that Christians reflect His character in their lives, which the Holy Spirit empowers believers to do through the purity of His holiness. Evans notes, "Since holiness is such a foreign concept to the human heart, ask God to help you to live each day in a healthy awareness of His awesome holiness. Pray that God will make the truth of 1 Peter 1:15-16, 'Be holy yourselves also in all your behavior, because it is written, "You shall be holy, for I am holy,"' a reality in your heart and life."[80] Disciples have a Person living within them to expand their understanding of what it means to be holy. Holiness is the sign and seal of God's presence in the world. God's holiness is also more than personal holiness. The Holy Spirit's presence should challenge and transform the society in which we live. The Holy Spirit is not eradicating sin in disciples' lives, but it gives them the power

---

[80] Tony Evans, *Our God is Awesome* (Chicago: Moody Press, 1994), 87.

to overcome the temptation of sin in their lives. The Holy Spirit has the power to transform the whole structure of culture and society. Moreover, holiness is not only personal and social; it is also missional. The Holy Spirit helps disciples to think in missional ways about the world and how they can mirror God's actions in the world.

The book of Acts also revealed how the disciples were persecuted for proclaiming the gospel of Jesus Christ. The gains the Christians were making were too great for the Jewish authorities to tolerate. Jerusalem was a relatively small city; but through the disciple's efforts, natives and visitors alike were being converted. Consequently, the high priest and the dominant Sadducees of the Sanhedrin met and the apostles were sent to be tried, but they could not be found in the prison. The angel of the Lord had intervened and set them free. They were right back where they were when they had been arrested, in the very temple itself, teaching the people. They were brought in without resistance to the Sanhedrin, and the high priest indignantly accused them of doing precisely what he had commanded them not to do, that is, teaching "in this name." He deliberately did not mention the name "Jesus." He did say, however, that it was the purpose of the apostles to bring "this man's blood" upon them. But what else could have been expected? Had they not said to Pilate, when he washed his hands of the guilt of condemning Jesus, "His blood be on us, and on our children" (Matthew 27:24)? That is exactly what the apostles reminded them of, as they said through Peter, "We ought to obey God rather than men" (5:29). Peter also stated that Jesus, whom they killed, God has highly exalted and made to be a Prince and a Savior in order to bring Israel to repentance and to offer the Jews the forgiveness of their sins. The apostles asserted that they and the Holy Spirit were witnesses to all the claims of Jesus. Luke was the first person in the New Testament to call Jesus "Savior." He used this word to describe Jesus only once in his Gospel (Luke 2:11), and in the book of Acts, he used it a second time by quoting Peter in his defense of himself and the other apostles before the Sanhedrin.

After Peter's testimony, the assembly went into rage and wanted to execute all of them. But Gamaliel, one of the greatest Hebrew rabbis and a member of the Pharisees, cautioned them against abrupt actions. He simply said that if they were mistaken fanatics, they would in the end destroy themselves. But if their message was true and what they did was inspired by God, there was really nothing the Sanhedrin could do about it, for God always triumphs. So the Sanhedrin was content to beat the apostles with a whip, order them again not to speak in the name of Jesus, and then let them go. The apostles counted themselves fortunate to be able to suffer for Jesus.

The church in Jerusalem had grown so large that the apostles could not handle its business and evangelize and nourish the flock spiritually. Administrative duties distracted them from prayer and the preaching of the word. At the same time, there is a complaint of the Grecians against the Hebrews because their widows were being neglected in the daily distribution. This was not a clash between two races. The word *Grecians* here means "Hellenists," Greek-speaking Jews. They had a background in Greek culture, while the Hebrews in Jerusalem closely followed the Mosaic Law, which naturally brought about a misunderstanding. To solve this problem, the congregation elected seven men of exemplary character to take on these administrative duties. In fact, Luke gives the criteria for these men who were chosen: "Therefore, brethren, seek out from among you seven men of good reputation, full of the Holy Spirit and wisdom whom we may appoint over this business" (Luke 6:3). The remarkable thing is that the congregation chose persons from the group that made the complaint. The seven, as their names indicate, were all Hellenized Jews. These men stood before the apostles who laid their hands on them after prayer and thereby set them apart for this task.

This short passage in Acts is crucial to an understanding of the development of ministry in the church. The apostles were the leaders of the church. They had been chosen by Jesus Himself at the very beginning of His earthly ministry, and followed Him throughout His earthly ministry. They were witnesses to His resurrection. The newly chosen servant-leaders were to be servants of the apostles, transacting business and performing administrative duties assigned to them. Although they had been elected by the congregation, they could not take office and begin their duties until after the apostles had prayed over them and laid their hands on their heads. The laying on of hands after prayer was the sign of the impartation of the Holy Spirit. Leroy Eims wrote, "Admittedly, it should be someone's job to serve food, but it was the apostles' job to serve or minister the word. Some of the disciples were to serve that which fed the body, while the apostles served that which fed the soul."[81] The disciples said, "But we will give ourselves continually to prayer and to the ministry of the word" (Acts 6:4). The apostles stuck to preaching the Word, the dispute got settled, and the church continued to explode with growth. Reiner notes that one of the weapons of Satan is distraction: "He attempts to divert the apostles from their calling of prayer and preaching by creating a problem of social administration (Acts 6:1-7). At each point when Satan attacks and the church overcomes, a new wave of revival floods the church: 'So the word of God spread. The number of disciples in Jerusalem increased rapidly. . .'" (Acts 6:7).[82]

---

[81] Leroy Eims, *Disciples in Action* (Colorado Springs: Navpress, 1981), 79.
[82] Rainer, 61.

> *In the twenty-first century, Satan will do everything he can to distract ministers by putting barriers in their way to hinder them from proclaiming the Word to God.*

In the twenty-first century, Satan will do everything he can to distract ministers by putting barriers in their way to hinder them from proclaiming the Word to God. The pastor cannot do the work of the ministry alone. There must be anointed disciples who assist the pastor in the work of the ministry. If the congregation is to be unified and operates as a team, then the disciples of Jesus Christ must model that unity and oneness of purpose among themselves. Evans wrote, "Conflicts are quickly resolved, unity is maintained, and its impact increases tremendously because its people are carrying out God's chosen agenda for the church."[83]

Actually, these seven were never called "deacons," but are considered to be the antecedents of the officers later referred to as "deacons." Luke describes in this short passage the origin of the diaconate (Acts 6:1-6), which was the church's second ministerial order. Up until that point, the apostolate had been the only ministerial order. When the apostles set these seven persons apart for their ministry of service, they performed for

---

[83] Tony Evans, *What a Way to Live,* 329.

the first time the sacred rite of ordination. That is not to say, however, that because their duties were primarily administrative and functional, they were inferior and had no spiritual quality. The first deacons preached as well. One of them, Stephen, performed miracles with the apostles themselves in the high quality of his ministry. In fact, he infuriated the leaders of several Hellenized synagogues in Jerusalem because he overshadowed them in debate. Since they could not get the better of him at argumentation, they lied about him, contending that he disparaged both the law and the Temple and thereby blasphemed Moses and God. As a result, he was brought before the Sanhedrin. Cannon wrote,

> In response to the questioning of the high priest, Stephen delivered the longest address recorded in the New Testament other than our Lord's Sermon on the Mount. He turned the tables on his accusers by saying that they had blasphemed Moses by not keeping his law and had defamed the name of God by presuming that God, like some man-made idol, can be confined to a building made of stone. It must have angered the Jewish leaders when Stephen reminded them that Joseph was buried in Shechem among the Samaritans, whom they despised. His review of history was a critical denunciation of Jewish apostasy, and according to his speech, what the Israelites had been, they

were still. He denounced the Sanhedrin for both idolatry and Temple worship. He spoke passionately, as if he were reliving the events he recounted. Luke says his face was like that of an angel.[84]

When Stephen told the Jewish leaders that they were stiff-necked and uncircumcised in heart and ears and that they resisted the Holy Spirit as their fathers had done, it was more than they could take. Henry wrote, "They like their fathers, were stubborn and willful, and would not be wrought upon by the various methods God took to reclaim and return them; they were like their fathers, inflexible both to the Word of God and to His providences."[85] They gnashed their teeth in rage. Stephen lifted his eyes toward heaven and cried out, "I see the heavens opened, and the Son of man standing on the right hand of God" (Acts 7:56). With that, the Jewish leaders rushed him and cast him out of the city and stoned him to death. In the process of throwing the stones, they placed their outer garments at the feet of a young man named Saul. Stephen died, asking God not to lay the sin of murder to the charge of them who slew him. By his death, he became the first martyr of the Christian church. Krodel wrote, "Stephen's martyrdom led to a general persecution in which Saul was most active, 'dragging

---

[84] Cannon, 47.
[85] Henry, 72.

men and women . . . to prison' (8:3). All 'except the apostles' were scattered from Jerusalem throughout Judea and Samaria where the subsequent action would take place."[86] Saul, for example went from house to house seeking out the Christians, throwing them into prison. Most of the Christians left Jerusalem and sought safety in Judea and Samaria. The apostles, however, stayed in their post of duty with the mother church. This scattering of Christians meant at the same time the dissemination of the gospel. Reiner wrote, "The martyrdom of Stephen (7:54-60) does not reduce the church to a level of frightened ineffectiveness. To the contrary, the persecution that broke out against the disciples scattered the church throughout Judea and Samaria. The defeated church then became the proclaiming church as the dispersion spread the gospel to new areas. God in his sovereignty turned defeat into a larger victory (8:4)."[87] They carried their faith with them and gave it to others wherever they went. The blood of the martyrs became the seed of the church. In this twenty-first century, disciples of Jesus Christ, like Stephen, must be able to speak both truth and grace. Stephen was able to speak the truth to the religious leaders, calling them heartless murderers and at the same time praying for their forgiveness (grace) as he was being stoned. It was as if Stephen were repeating what Jesus said on the cross,

---

[86] Gerhard Krodel, *Acts Proclamation Commentaries* (Philadelphia: Fortress Press, 1981), 34.
[87] Rainer, 62.

"Father, forgive them, for they do not know what they do" (Luke 23:34).

A great example of the power of the Holy Spirit is exhibited in the witness of Peter and John in Acts chapter three. After Pentecost, the disciples began to perform miracles and spread the gospel of Jesus Christ. Peter and John went to the temple at the time of prayer and they encountered a man who had been lame from birth. Brought to the Beautiful Gate daily, this beggar asked Peter and John for some money. Peter looked at this man and said, "Silver and gold have I none; but such as I have give I thee: In the name of Jesus Christ of Nazareth rise up and walk. And he took him by the right hand, and lifted him up: and immediately his feet and ankle bones received strength" (Acts 3:6-7). The lame man jumped up, stood on his feet, and began to walk, leap, and praise God. He then entered the temple with them. Imagine how many people had simply ignored this beggar each day. Many people who see someone who looks a little different or undesirable, go out of their way not to come near that person. Maybe there were some who were not offended or put off by this man, but they simply did not have or take the time to deal with him. Peter and John made the effort to reach this man personally. And when Peter and John encountered him, they "fastened their eyes on him" (Acts 3:4). In this twenty-first century, disciples of Jesus Christ must make every effort to reach people personally. It will not be enough to expect them to just walk into the church doors on Sunday. The best chance a disciple has to lead someone to Jesus is to develop a personal relationship with that person.

The disciples also reached people publicly. After this miracle, the people saw this beggar walking and praising God. The crowd was astonished and amazed! Peter saw and immediately addressed the crowd. Peter made it clear that this miracle was not through his own power. Peter and John preached Jesus! He told them that he and John did nothing, but it was God who did it. Peter boldly proclaimed that this man was healed through faith in the name of God's Son, Jesus, whom they had rejected. Peter goes on to tell them in Acts 3:19, "Repent ye therefore, and be converted, that your sins may be blotted out, when the times of refreshing shall come from the presence of the Lord." In this twenty-first century, disciples of Jesus Christ must boldly share the same message that Peter proclaimed back in the first century. They are to reach people personally, but never pass up the opportunity to testify publicly. Being a disciple is not about personal fame and glory, but about obedience and God's glory. Peter and John publicly "preached through Jesus the resurrection from the dead" (Acts 4:2). In fact, chapter three can be summarized as: God sent Jesus, Jesus was rejected, Jesus died for your sins, and repent of your sins.

After the miracle and the message came persecution! They were seized and held overnight. The next day they were brought before Annas the high priest as well as Caiaphas and others. Peter and John were asked by the council what power enabled them to do this. They answered by saying that it was Jesus of Nazareth, whom they crucified, who healed this man. Peter then boldly proclaimed, "Nor is there salvation in any other, for there is no other name under heaven given among men by which we must be saved" (Acts 4:12). The council was astonished by the boldness of Peter and John, especially noticing that they were uneducated and untrained, and they had been with Jesus. The keyword in this text is "boldness." They did not compromise, and they did not fear imprisonment or death. They were determined to stand firm and speak the truth. In fact, they used their persecution as another opportunity to proclaim the gospel. In this twenty-first century, disciples of Jesus Christ will encounter persecution, but they must be determined to remain bold and firm in the face of it. Disciples are called to be both faithful and fruitful. In the Gospel of John, Jesus said, "You did not choose Me, but I chose you and appointed you that you should go and bear fruit, and *that* your fruit should remain, that whatever you ask the Father in My name He may give you" (John 15:16). Fruitful disciples are a rare breed in the twenty-first century.

What is the result of being a fruitful disciple? Lives will be changed. "However, many of those who heard the word believed; and the number of the men came to be about five thousand" (Acts 4:4). How amazing it must have been to witness this man who had been lame since birth begin to walk, leap and praise the Lord. What a blessing for Peter and John to witness a life being changed. In this twenty-first century, disciples of Jesus Christ have the same opportunity as Peter and John to be vessels used by God to change people's lives spiritually. The Holy Spirit combined with the preached Word of God will bring about spiritual deliverance in the lives of many. For the disciples to attempt to do anything without the Word of God would have been an exercise in futility. Paul said, "How then shall they call on Him in whom they have not believed? And how shall they believe in Him of whom they have not heard? And how shall they hear without a preacher?" (Romans 10:14). It is the Word that reveals sin, demands repentance and points people to Jesus as being "the way, the truth, and the life" (John 14:6).

The people to whom Peter and John ministered responded to the Word. In fact, "the number of the men came to be about five thousand" (Acts 4:4). Not only did they hear, but a great number believed. This all started when Peter and John took the time to heal a lame beggar. They went from this lame beggar, to the crowd, and to the religious rulers. God had orchestrated the perfect plan. Disciples of Jesus Christ can be assured that God's plan will be blessed. They may attempt to do a work for the Lord, and it may seem to them that they failed. It may have seemed this way to Peter and John as they were seized and held overnight. In this twenty-first century, disciples of Jesus Christ can rest assured that if they remain faithful and fruitful, God will use them to do great things for His name's sake. Many people out there are in the same condition as this beggar. They are lame spiritually. They can't help themselves. They may be looking for something and they just don't know what it is. Disciples know that special Someone whom everybody needs, and His name if Jesus. Jesus is the source of physical and spiritual healing.

Chapter nine of the book of Acts describes the conversion of Saul on the Damascus Road. Saul was breathing out threats and murder against the disciples of the Lord and to the high priest to ask him for letters to the synagogues in Damascus, so that if he found anyone belonging to Christ, men or women, he would bring them bound to Jerusalem. But as he approached Damascus, a light shined around him, and falling to the ground he heard a voice say to him, "Saul, Saul, why are you persecuting me?"

Saul responded, "Who are you, Lord?"

And the voice said, "I am Jesus, whom you are persecuting. But rise and enter the city, and you will be told what you are to do" (Acts 9:5-6). In an instant, the accuser became the accused. Before Saul could reach Damascus, he was struck down by a blinding light and told by a voice from heaven that he was an enemy of God engaged in warfare against God's own people. Saul recognized the voice as carrying divine authority and there was no doubt in his mind about this. And the voice accused him of persecuting the very One who was speaking to him. When Saul asked for an identification, the speaker identified Himself as Jesus. Saul perceived that the One he had hated and despised as an evil impostor was the true Messiah and was now in heaven in the presence of God. He realized with fear and trembling that in persecuting the followers of Jesus, he was persecuting Jesus and, through Him, almighty God. The men who were travelling with him were speechless, because they heard, but saw no one. Saul got up from the ground, and though his eyes were open, he also saw nothing. They led him by the hand and brought him into Damascus, and for three days he was without sight, and neither ate nor drank anything.

The Lord gave Ananias, a disciple in Damascus, instructions to go to Straight Street, and ask for a man from Tarsus name Saul, to whom God gave a vision that Ananias would be coming and laying hands on him so that he might regain his sight. Ananias shared with Jesus that he had heard about Saul and how much evil he had done to the saints Jerusalem, and that he had authority from the chief priests to bind all who called upon His name. But the Lord instructed Ananias to do as He commanded, for Saul was chosen as an instrument to carry out the name of Jesus before the Gentiles, kings, and the children of Israel. Jesus noted that He would show Saul how much he would suffer for His name's sake. Therefore, Ananias departed, as the Lord instructed, and entered the house. And laying hands on Saul, Ananias said, "Brother Saul, the Lord Jesus who appeared to you on the road by which you came has sent me so that you may regain your sight and be filled with the Holy Spirit" (Acts 9:17). Immediately something like scales fell from Saul's eyes, and he regained his sight. After he arose and was baptized, he ate food and received his strength.

For many days, he was with the disciples in Damascus proclaiming Jesus in the synagogues as the Son of God. Everyone was amazed, wondering if this was the same man who had been persecuting Christians, and if he had come to bring them before the chief priests. Even with all the doubters, Saul increased in his strength, proving to the Jews in Damascus that Jesus was the Christ. After many days had passed, the Jews plotted to kill him, but he was able to escape. And when he went to Jerusalem, he attempted to join the disciples, but they were afraid of him, because they did not believe that he was a disciple. But Barnabas brought him to the apostles, declared to them that he had been converted, and preached boldly in the name of

Jesus. As he was preaching, he argued with the Hellenists, who were seeking to kill him. And when the brothers heard about this, they brought him down to Caesarea and sent him off to Tarsus. In the midst of all that Saul was facing, the church throughout all Judea, Galilee and Samaria had peace and was being built up in the faith. The church multiplied as a result of walking in the fear of the Lord and in the comfort of the Holy Spirit. From Acts 13 forward, Saul became the Apostle Paul. The apostle Paul had a wonderful testimony to share as he went about his missionary journeys. In fact, he shared his conversion experience before King Agrippa in Acts 26. His testimony was so powerful that King Agrippa said to Paul, "You almost persuade me to become a Christian" (Acts 26:28). In this twenty-first century, disciples of Jesus Christ must be transparent and eager to share their testimony about what the Lord has done in their lives. The world needs to know that disciples of Jesus Christ have not always been saved. The same work that God did in their lives, He can do in the life of someone else.

In conclusion, there is another story of the great devotion of two disciples in Acts chapter sixteen that should inspire twenty-first century disciples today. In the midst of persecution, a disciple can still have joy even when it does not make sense. James said, "My brethren, count it all joy when you fall into various trials" (James 1:2). Paul and Silas were ministering when they were arrested. They were in prison because they cast the spirit out of a slave girl who was being used by her owners to make money for fortune telling. She earned a great deal of money for her owners. Paul simply said, "In the name of Jesus Christ I command you to come out of her!" (Acts 16:13). At that moment the spirit left her. When the owners realized that their hope of making money was gone, they seized Paul and Silas and dragged them into the marketplace to face the authorities, even though they really had done nothing wrong. All they had done was preach the love of Jesus and heal a demon-possessed girl. Still, they were mistreated, abused, beaten and imprisoned. They could have responded with verbal threats and curses from the inner cell or they could have responded by saying, "They have no right to treat me like this. It is not right. It is not fair." But this is not how they responded. Luke says that "at midnight Paul and Silas were praying and singing hymns to God, and the other prisoners were listening to them" (Acts 16:25). Paul and Silas had been stripped, beaten, and thrown into the very darkest cell in the prison and fastened in stocks. And what do they do? They prayed, sang, and had a mini-revival in their cell. They could have allowed their situation to take control of them. But instead, they took control of their own situation by rejoicing in God. The end result was that Paul and Silas witnessed to a literal captive audience. The Philippian jailer and his family were saved and baptized in the name of Jesus.

In this twenty-first century, disciples of Jesus Christ will be confronted with various trials and tribulations, but if they will allow the Holy Spirit to lead and guide them, God can use trials and tribulations to accomplish some great things to His glory and honor. Paul said, "And we know that all things work together for good to those who love God, to those who are the called according to His purpose" (Romans 8:28). In addition, they will find peace and joy in the Holy Spirit. When non-believers see disciples of Jesus Christ praising the Lord in the midst of life's storms, it will encourage them to want the God of the disciples. This story also demonstrates the importance of the power of prayer. Rainer notes, "Churches today must place a priority on prayer which will be evident in their programs, budget, and calendar. The early church viewed prayer as the very life source of everything they did. Prayer was not the leader in a series of programs; it was the foundation upon which all other ministry was built. Prayer was vitally important because the believers in Acts realized that their battles were to be fought in the spiritual realm.[88] Chapter five will explore discipleship in the twenty-first century, and discuss the reasons why traditional churches are not growing.

---

[88] Rainer, 67.

CHAPTER FOUR

EXPLORE DISCIPLESHIP IN THE TWENTY-FIRST CENTURY

I n this chapter, there will be an exploration of discipleship in the twenty-first century, and a discussion of the
reasons why churches are declining. The facts truly support the idea of the church's decline.

A new Gallup poll survey finds that U.S. church membership has fallen below a majority for the first time in nearly a
century. For the first time in 80 years of surveys, Americans'
membership in houses of worship dropped below 50 percent.
A survey by Gallup finds that in 2020, 47 percent of Americans said they belonged to a church, synagogue, or mosque,
down from 50 percent in 2018 and 70 percent in 1999. When

Gallup first measured church membership in 1937, it was 73 percent. It remained near 70 percent for the next six decades, before beginning a steady decline around the turn of the millennium. Gallup also asks Americans numerous questions each year about their religious attitudes and practices. Some trends emerged in an analysis of declining church membership across three-year aggregates: 1998–2000 (when church membership averaged 69 percent), 2008–10 (62 percent), and 2018–20 (49 percent). The decline in church membership appears to be primarily a result of more Americans expressing no religious preference. For the past 20 years, the percentage of Americans who do not identify with any religion has grown from 8 percent in 1998–2000 to 13 percent in 2008–10, and 21 percent in the past three years. This trend appears to account for more than half of the 20-point decline in church membership during the same time. Most of the rest of the drop can be attributed to a decline in formal church membership among Americans who *do* have a religious preference. The decline in church membership, as Gallup notes, appears largely tied to population change. Those in older generations who were likely to be church members are being replaced in the U.S. adult population by younger people less likely to join institutions. About 66 percent of traditionalists (U.S. adults born before 1946) belong to a church, compared with 58 percent of baby boomers, 50 percent of those in Generation X, and 36 percent of millennials.[89]

Why is the church losing its influence? Why is the church losing its youth and young adults? Why is the church not growing numerically and even spiritually? This chapter will not serve as an exclusive answer to the problem, but it will look at some specific problems that have caused the decline in American churches and explore some discipleship solutions for the twenty-first century.

As noted in chapter one, the traditional church in America is in trouble. At one time, America was the main country sending missionaries throughout the world with the gospel. And now, America is an anti-Christian mission field. The problem facing the church today is all together deeper and more desperate than what faced the Christian church many years ago. Denis Lacorne wrote, "God was dead and nowhere was his absence more obvious than in America. Or, more precisely, a new pagan divinity had taken the place of the Christian God: "the almighty dollar," technology, mechanization, or mass production."[90]

---

[89] Joe Carter, *"Why is Church Membership in America on the Decline,"* The Gospel Coalition, March 31, 2021. Internet available at: Why Is Church Membership in America on the Decline? (thegospel-coalition.org)
[90] Denis Lacorne, *"Religion in America: A Political History,"* New York: Columbia University Press, 1988:104. Internet available at:
http://search.ebscohost.com/login.aspx?di-rect=true&AuthType=ip,uid&db=e000xna&AN=399886&site=ehost-live&scope=site

In Mark 9, as Jesus was coming down the mountain with Peter, James and John from the mount of transfiguration to gather with the other disciples, He saw a great multitude around them, and scribes disputing with them. Jesus then asked what was being discussed. Someone in the crowd said, "Teacher, I brought You my son, who has a mute spirit. And wherever it seizes him, it throws him down; he foams at the mouth, gnashes his teeth, and becomes rigid. So I spoke to Your disciples, that they should cast it out, but they could not" (Mark 9:17-18). So as the story goes, Jesus healed the man's son, and the demon spirit came out of him. Then the disciples asked Jesus privately why they could not cast it out. Jesus said, "This kind can come out by nothing but prayer and fasting" (Mark 9:29). In Timothy Keller's lecture, he quoted David Martyn Lloyd-Jones, who was a Welsh Protestant minister and medical doctor influential in the Reformed wing of the British evangelical movement in the twentieth century.

The demons are in too deep for churches to operate in an ordinary way.

The demons are in too deep for churches to operate in an ordinary way. The ordinary way they operate will not work with today's demons. How do disciples get people back to attending traditional churches in this twenty-first century, especially the Generation X (born between 1964 and 1979), the Generation Y or Millennials (born between 1980 and 1994), and Generation Z (born between 1995 and 2010)? The very future of twenty-first century churches will depend on reaching them over the next five to ten years. Ordinary traditional worship or evangelism outreach tools will not work anymore, because everyone seems to have some form of spirituality, even if it is the wrong spirit. The demons are in too deep. In the twenty-first century, there are three main reasons why the demons are in too deep.

First, there is a truth problem. All biblical truth claims are perceived as limitations or power plays and are seen as exclusive. You say to most people today that marriage "is between a man and a woman," and they will want to persecute you for your exclusiveness. You say to them, "Jesus is the only way to heaven," you may have a fight on your hands, and yet that is exactly what Jesus said when he said in John 14:6, "no man comes to the father but by me." No one seems to want to hear about absolutes anymore. Steve McSwain made these powerful statements about absolutes and the twenty-first century church: "My own feeling is, however, the 21st Century Church future lies in offering "absolutes" to young people who do need boundaries within which to safely forge a real-world faith.

Those boundaries, however, must be grounded in facts, in honest inquiry, and in intellectual integrity."[91]

Second, there is a guilt problem. Sometimes when ministers are preaching or teaching, they assume a consciousness of guilt from the congregation. They assume that the listeners know that they ought to be good. They assume that they know that the Word of God is the absolute truth and that somehow, they know that they need to be good, decent people. And today, that is not the case. Things that baby boomers would have been ashamed to do forty or fifty years ago, do not bother young people today. For example, many baby boomers grew up during a time when it was frowned upon to live together before marriage, but in the twenty-first century it seems to be the norm. There is no consciousness of guilt.

Third, there is a meaning problem. Many people don't believe that biblical words or texts can get across too many people today. Here is a biblical text. Whose interpretation is correct? Meanings are unstable, which makes it challenging for preachers to preach the gospel to these twenty-first century generations. To make matters worse, interpretations are much more confusing if pastors and teachers are not properly trained and prepared to present the gospel.

---

[91] Steve McSwain, "*21ˢᵗ Century Church: New Absolutes the Church must Embrace or Die,*" The Huffington Post, Dec. 6, 2017. Internet available at: <u>21st Century Church: New Absolutes the Church Must Embrace or Die (Part 1) | HuffPost</u>

So how can disciples be assured that the institution of the church will still exist for many years to come? How can the church be more effective in making disciples in the twenty-first century?

First, the church of Jesus Christ must understand congregational ecology. Congregational ecology refers to the things that happen outside a congregation that can shape what happens inside a congregation. It is the world beyond the congregation. Nancy Eiesland and R. Stephen Warner said, "Even as it is dedicated to God, your congregation is a human institution located in history (the date of its founding to the present), in a specific place in geography (your community), and in the lives of its members (the network "maps" of their lives). We call this time-space-network location the context of the congregation."[92] Congregational ecology involves looking at the neighborhood. Is the church in a residential or commercial district? What are the current demographics of the church? When learning about the congregation, it is always important to take stock of the population in the area around you. Demographics shift; and when a congregation relies on only one demographic, these shifts can mean big changes for the congregation. What is the current age, ethnicity and class of the congregation? Congregational ecology looks at how a mega church in the area can

---

[92] Nancy Eiesland and R. Stephen Warner, *Studying Congregation* (Nashville: Abingdon Press, 1998), 43.

impact a congregation. Congregations are voluntary associations and sometimes other options nearby can shape the life of a congregation. Congregational ecology looks at the surrounding rural, suburban and urban environments which can shape a congregation in all kinds of ways. Quite often, proximity to locations where various ethnic groups have settled can shape a congregation. Congregational ecology looks at social issues that may shape a congregation, such as the civil rights movement in the 1960s, which impacted many church congregations. In this twenty-first century, new movements such as gay rights, social injustices and pro-life movements will have an impact on church congregations. Congregational ecology involves networking with like-minded communities such as other denominations, associations and informal partnerships. It might also include relationships with theological schools or other educational institutions. This COVID-19 Pandemic has caused many leaders of local congregations to learn new skills. Worship services, Bible studies, and committee meetings are via Zoom and Facebook. Phone calls have replaced home visitation for sick and shut-in members. Food distribution points have been set up at various churches to meet the need of families. Congregations are continuing to serve even with empty church pews. The church will never be the same even after the Pandemic. Congregational ecology can also shape a congregation based on national trends and national narratives. For example, American congregations have shaped stories about the founding of the country and its status as a so-called "Christian" nation. Congregational ecology takes into account the things that happen on the outside of the congregation that mold and shape what happens on the inside of the congregation. In this twenty-first century, it will be very difficult for disciples to make disciples if they do not understand the importance of congregational ecology and the demographics of the church community.

Second, if disciples are going to make disciples, they need to understand the characteristics of the modern generations from which new disciples will be drawn. The primary generations that make up a society today are the Traditionalists, or Silent Generation (born 1945 and before), baby boomers (born between 1946 – 1964), Generation X (born between 1965 – 1980), Millennials or Generation Y (born between 1981 – 1994), and Generation Z (born between 1995 – 2010). For this book, the main focus will be on Generation X, Y, and Z.

Generation X was born between 1965 and 1980. This generation is skeptical of authority and tends not to respect hierarchy, status or title. People in this generation seek work-life balance and prefer an informal, fun workplace. Typical characteristics of a Generation X workplace would focus on self-reliance, individual projects and minimal supervision. This generation is not interested in spending hours in meetings;

instead, Gen Xers demand high productivity and prefer to complete tasks as quickly as possible to free up more personal time. They are looking to purchase homes and start a family. Regardless of their spending habits, they value saving money through retirement accounts, such as 401Ks. They are likely to have an emergency fund. This group holds the highest employment rate of any generation, according to the Bureau of Labor Statistics. They also are more knowledgeable of their risk tolerance. While Baby Boomers are downgrading their homes as they age out of the workforce and retire, people in Generation X are heavily focused on making a comfortable home for themselves. Purchasing a home in an area with a good school district is the ideal. Many members of Generation X believe that job security comes from being their own boss. Instead of hoping to find employment, people in this generation show a willingness to take control of the future by investing in their careers, which gives them an opportunity to succeed in professions about which they are passionate. Generation X was the first generation to be defined by its heavy use of technology. People in this generation crave information and rely on themselves to solve personal challenges with the aid of the internet. Generation X consumers are also looking to compare prices, see pictures, and explore social media activity. Online "window shopping" must offer easy navigation to encourage a sale as well. They have been labeled as skeptics for their unwillingness to accept things at face value. As such, they may be less receptive to traditional sales pitches or gimmicks than other generations. Generation X tends to make purchasing decisions based on research and has more appreciation for companies that offer transparency in their practices and products. Gen Xers believe in sex before marriage, but not the free sex that was practiced during the baby boom era, probably because of the danger of HIV/AIDS. Generation X is also known as the divorce generation. Couples tend to break up rather than work together through relationship problems like previous generations. Because there is not the same social stigma about divorce, it has become the easiest option. Generation X tends to respect parents less than previous generations.[93]

Generation Y, also known as the Millennial Generation, was born between 1981 and 2006. Millennials are a very diverse and progressive group whose values are very different than previous generations. They are characterized by limited identification with any political group. Millennials are the most diverse of all the generational groups – one in three is a minority. They are optimistic, confident, civic-minded and fully committed to moral and ethical principles. This generation expects full communication, speedy decision-making and requires information to be available immediately. Characteristics of a

---

[93] Eugene Chrinian, *"Top Characteristics of Generation X Consumers,"* May 3, 2016. Internet available at: 7 of the Top Characteristics of Generation X Consumers | Eugene Chrinian (wordpress.com)

Generation Y workplace include constant e-mail communications, multitasking and a recognition that work is a means to an end. Millennials are much less likely that older Americans to pray or attend church regularly or to consider religion an important part of their lives. The Millennial is more racially diverse than previous generations and represents a shift in family values and structure. Millennials are from more non-traditional families than earlier generations, and are from more frequently single parents, cohabiting and unmarried with children or married without children. They embrace progressive views more than they affiliate with political parties. They differ from previous generations in their support of cooperative foreign policy and universal health care. Millennials are more likely to feel positively about immigration and support a clear path to citizenship for undocumented immigrants. Religious affiliation is declining among them. They represent changing attitudes toward social issues. They are more supportive of gay marriage, and perceive racial and gender equality as socially given. Millennials have the highest education level in American history.[94] They were born into an emerging world of technology and have grown up surrounded by smart phones, laptops, tablets and other gadgets. Technology is an essential aspect of their lives. They will reply more quickly to an email,

---

[94] Agatha Clark, *"Millennial Generation Characteristics,"* Agatha Clark, September 29, 2017. Internet available at: Millennial Generation Characteristics (synonym.com)

tweet, or Facebook message than to a phone call. To Millennials, media is powerful, but social media is more powerful. The impact Millennials have already made through media and social media is undeniable. The grassroots movements that take place in the social media world are amazing. Rainer said, "Millennials that disagree with the practices or products of a company can stage a boycott that can disrupt multimillion-dollar industries. It takes just one group or event on Facebook to cause CEOs to shake their heads in wonder."[95] Generation Y is also attracted to organizations where technology is top priority. Traditional companies are less of an attraction for the millennial generation. Millennials want to work for progressive companies who are embracing these new means of communication and implementing them into business as opposed to organizations with a more traditional mindset. Technology needs to be an integral part of this generation's day-to-day life. Instead of working long hours to work their way up an organization, Millennials prefer flexible working schedules and a more rounded work/life balance. This generation prefers to work to live, not live to work. Family life takes priority over the work place. They have seen their parents live to work, which has driven their new perception. The Millennials just want the best mix of an enjoyable life and fulfilling work. They are

---

[95] Thom S. Rainer and Jess W. Rainer, *The Millennials* (Nashville: B&H Publishing Group, 2011), 201.

confident and ambitious. Expectations typically need to be managed as Millennials are confident to take on important roles within organizations as soon as they begin. With young entrepreneurs like Mark Zuckerberg, Millennials believe that there is no limit to what they can achieve. Millennials have high expectations of their employees and expect this to be matched. Many are not afraid to seek employment elsewhere if this ambition is not met. Unlike generations before them, they are happy to change roles more often to find the right organizations. Teamwork is high on the agenda of Millennials to include regular team meetings and collaboration with colleagues. Millennials want to be involved and included. They expect openness and transparency from management and colleagues and seek a team-playing mentality within an organization. Communication is key for Millennials; however, it has to be on the right terms. Constant feedback and gratitude are common expectations. In previous generations, this level of communication was unheard of with senior management; however, Millennials in the workplace seek this level of feedback. Companies have begun to implement mentor schemes to develop and guide Millennials in their careers. Having this level of guidance and reassurance is essential when working with and nurturing this generation. This generation is the fastest growing generation in business and business leaders. Love them or hate them, this generation is here to stay and will continue to make advancements within business.[96]

Generation Z describes people who were born between 1995 and 2010. For many years, the church has been focusing on attracting Millennials, but a new generation of adults is emerging with its own identity. This generation has grown up connected to the web and social media. Generation Z wants to be constantly connected to friends and have the ability to chat anywhere, anytime, at an early age. This increased exposure to social media has brought some unwanted consequences. Many people of this generation say social media impacts their self-esteem. If the church wants to leverage social media to reach Generation Z, it will have to spend time on social platforms that the next generation uses. Having a Facebook page will not be enough to stay connected to young adults. In this twenty-first century, the church should focus on helping teens find their identity and self-worth in Christ, not in the online opinion of others. Generation Z makes up one-third of the population of the United States. For the church to move forward, it must reach this new generation. Here are eight unique characteristics of this young generation and why Generation Z should matter to the Church today. People who belong to this generation grew up after the advent of home computers

---

[96] GAIA Insights, *"Generation Y Characteristics,"* Jan. 2019. Internet available at: Generation Y Characteristics – Generation Y

and the internet. They do not remember life before laptops, cellphones, iPads and iPods. These things have always been there! That means today's young people are used to constant change. Change is simply a way of life for them — and they handle those changes well.[97] James Emery White says, "The speed by which this technological revolution has taken place is stunning and makes it difficult for older generations to realize the radically different world into which Generation Z has been born."[98] They're looking for the local church to keep up with changing times as skillfully as the apps on their phone that update weekly. This generation is used to always-on internet and making high-definition videos on smart phones. But it is not all about technology for Generation Z. People who belong to this generation view texting and social media as a tool to arrange meet-ups later with close friends. Because they have been schooled on the dangers of online threats, they would rather develop friendships in person. That means they are more likely to have real, lasting relationships. Growing up during the Great Recession has had a profound effect on Generation Z. Instead of chasing meaningful work, they are more interested in the security of a good job. Because of that, they are more willing to work hard and meet the expectations of employers. They are highly motivated in their work, but that does not

---

[97] King of Glory AG (n.d), *"Eight Characteristics of Generation Z,"* Internet available at: <u>Eight Characteristics of Generation Z – kingofgloryag.org</u>

[98] James Emery White, *Meet Generation Z* (Grand Rapids: Baker Books, 2017), 42.

mean they are unwilling to take a low-level job and stay there. Many in this generation want to start their own business. The parents of Generation Z gave their children more space. As a result, these young people can take on a task and deliver on deadlines with little to no checking in. Diversity is a default setting for Generation Z. Older generations may notice when the room is diverse, but Generation Z will notice if it is not diverse enough. Millennials and Generation Zs are the most racially diverse generations.[99]

Tom Rainer and Jess Rainer observations about Millennials apply to Generation Z as well: "We are not forced to have friends of varying backgrounds; instead, these relationships naturally form regardless of race or ethnicity. Diversity is not an issue for Millennials. We do not feel a need to be diverse, and we do not seek out relationships for that purpose. It is just who we are. We are diverse."[100] The need for church to become multicultural is only going to increase as Generation Z enters adulthood. Being surrounded by people from different ethnicities and cultures is becoming the norm for this generation. White says this about Generation Z: "They are growing up in a post-911 world. They are experiencing radical changes in technology and understandings of family, sexuality, and gender.

---

[99] King of Glory AG (n.d), Internet available at: Eight Characteristics of Generation Z – kingofgloryag.org
[100] Rainer and Rainer, 36.

They live in multigenerational households, and the fastest growing demographics within their age group is multiracial."[101] That means they are globally minded, more likely to support world missions, and eager to reach a wider audience in their church. As the church grows, it will find more things that separate Generation Z members from past generations and prepare them to meet the challenges of the future head-on. White further states, "As the first truly post-Christian generation, and numerically the largest, Generation Z will be the most influential religious force in the West and the heart of the missional challenge facing the Christian church."[102] To complicate the matter, Generation Z is focused on self. People who belong to this generation put emphasis on excessive individuality, and believe that the first goal of life is to be true to self. They are very self-focused. Jean Twenge said, "GenMe's focus on the needs of the individual is not necessarily self-absorbed or isolationist; instead, it's a way of moving through the world beholden to few social rules and with the unshakable belief that you're important."[103] Millennials and Generation Z have dramatically impacted the modern-day culture. Timothy Keller said, "If we are not deliberately thinking about our culture, we will be conformed to it without ever knowing it is happening."[104]

---

[101] White, 39.
[102] Ibid., 11.
[103] Twenge, 63.
[104] Timothy Keller, *Center Church* (Grand Rapids: Zondervan), 186.

Once the church understands congregational ecology and the characteristics of the different generations, disciples of Jesus Christ can effectively go and make new disciples.

Once the church understands congregational ecology and the characteristics of the different generations, disciples of Jesus Christ can effectively go and make new disciples. Because the very existence of the future of the church will depend on reaching these primary generations over the next five to ten years, what should the church do to reach these diverse generations of people?

First, disciples must be authentic and real about who they are. Disciples of Jesus Christ need to be authentic about reaching unbelievers of all generations. Most Millennial Christians see local churches as business-as-usual, focused inwardly, more concerned about the needs of the members than the needs of the community and the nations. Thom S. Rainer says this about how Millennial Christians view community: "Millennial Christians will reject churches that tend to view the community as little more than a population pool from which growth in attendance and budget can come. But they will embrace churches that teach members to love the community."[105] Millennials

---

[105] Rainer and Rainer, 261.

have little tolerance for churches that are hypocritical and do not embrace love for one another. Rainer makes note about an interesting and significant trend:

> Millennials tend to follow the examples of their parents in matters of faith, but they also tend to take the level of commitment one step further. For example, a Millennial with parents who were nominal Christians is likely to divorce himself of herself altogether from Christianity and churches. But a Millennial whose parents demonstrated some fervency in their Christian faith is likely to become more fervent. The bottom line is that most Millennials will not be lukewarm in their Christian faith. Most of them have made the decision not to embrace Christianity and to be forthright about their beliefs. Again, for them religion is not a major issue as it was with their parents. Many of their parents at least affirmed some level of Christian commitment. The Millennial children no longer will play that game. The vast majority is declaring that religion in general, and Christianity in particular, is not high on their list of priorities.[106]

Generations X, Y, and Z have high expectations of Christians being true to who they are, and will reject disciples and churches that are not authentic.

---

[106] Ibid., 245-246.

Second, disciples must build relationships. In many communities today there are a lot of dysfunctional families as the result of alcohol, drug addiction, divorce and unwed mothers. A dysfunctional family life is one of the leading causes of Millennials falling away from the church. A key to drawing Millennials closer to God is building genuine relationships with them and gaining their trust in the process. Reggie McNeal notes, "We have operated off the faulty assumption that if people participate in our church programs, they will grow and develop personally. Developing people requires building relationships, not just delivering a product or service."[107] Disciples have to love people, build relationships, and cultivate that trust. They need to do it with honesty and respect even if the unbeliever never comes to Christ. The more the culture drifts away from Christian values, the more a disciple must build a respectful relationship of trust with the unbeliever. And this must be done before the disciple can even hope to share any biblical content. Building relationships takes time. Energy must be put into it. This is a big reason why a large number of traditional congregations today are full of Baby Boomers only, because they must dig down deep in order to build lasting relationships with the younger generations. Maybe it is as simple as taking them out for pizza or bowling just to get to know

---

[107] Reggie McNeal, *Missional Renaissance: Changing the Scorecard for the Church* (Hoboken: John Riley & Sons, 2009), 67.

them better. **Paul said,** "For the whole law can be summed up in this one command: 'Love your neighbor as yourself'" (Galatians 5:14). **He further states in Ephesians 4:2,** "Always be humble and gentle. Be patient with each other, making allowance for each other's faults because of your love." The wisdom writer says in Proverbs 18:24, "A man *who has* friends must himself be friendly, but there is a friend *who* sticks closer than a brother."

Third, disciples must be transparent. The more transparent and vulnerable a disciple can be, the more Millennials connect. There was a time when speakers and teachers were told not to use themselves in personal illustrations; however, this generation wants to hear those personal stories. If disciples of Jesus Christ act as those who have it all together and not in desperate need of God's grace daily, they will lose credibility with the younger generations, who will either conclude that the disciples are not "being real" or that faith is unattainable for them. Transparency encourages people to open up more. In this twenty-first century, disciples of Jesus Christ need to ensure that they are transparent with Generations X, Y and Z.

In this twenty-first century, disciples of Jesus Christ need to ensure that they are transparent with Generations X, Y and Z.

Just recently on reality television, twenty-nine-year-old gospel singer, Kierra Sheard, gave an example of a fictional member of a church whose life experiences could help others: "I think in this church we have to be transparent. We have to be open because at the end of the day we're still questioning mothers on the front row who have five kids from five different men [but] we're not going to ask them [about it]," she said. "We're discussing it amongst ourselves [saying], 'well, she knows about sex. She knows what I'm struggling with because she's been with five different men, but she's the mother of the church.'"

When this type of person isn't transparent about his or her issues, Sheard believes younger people in the church start to question, "Why can we not talk to her about this?" The Millennials today want genuine transparency. Transparency does not mean that disciples have to share every detail about their personal lives, but they need to help others learn through their experiences. The purpose of disciples' transparency, openness, and honesty is not so they can describe all their trials and tribulations, but so they can describe how God saw them through their challenges. Rainer notes, "Transparent leaders are, to use the words of one Millennial, 'sincere men and women who don't have to wear a religious mask. We know that these leaders have the same challenges and struggles we do.'"[108] Paul notes this in Ephesians 4:25, "Therefore, having put away

---

[108] Rainer and Rainer, 268.

falsehood, let each one of you speak the truth with his neighbor, for we are members one of another." Paul further states, "For our boast is this, the testimony of our conscience, that we behaved in the world with simplicity and godly sincerity, not by earthly wisdom but by the grace of God, and supremely so toward you" (2 Corinthians 1:12).

Fourth, the church must have disciples who maintain humility and integrity. There is an increasing need for integrity in the ministry. Integrity involves character, ethics, and morals. Warren W. Wiersbe states, "We are facing an integrity crisis. Not only is the conduct of the church in question, but so is the very character of the church."[109] The *Oxford Advanced Learner's Dictionary* defines integrity as "the quality of being honest and having strong moral principles."[110] Henry Cloud said, "When we are talking about integrity, we are talking about being a whole person, an integrated person, with all of our different parts working well and delivering the functions that they were designed to deliver."[111] Leaders were designed to deliver the functions of the Word of God. The traits that hinder integrity in the man or woman of God are pride, materialism, arrogance, and exaggeration of accomplishments. David Canada

---

[109] Warren W. Wiersbe, *The Integrity Crisis* (Nashville: Thomas Nelson Publishers, 1988), 171.

[110] *Oxford Advanced Learners Dictionary*, Oxford University Press, 2021. Internet available at: integrity noun - Definition, pictures, pronunciation and usage notes | Oxford Advanced Learner's Dictionary at OxfordLearnersDictionaries.com

[111] Dr. Henry Cloud, *Integrity: the courage to meet the demands of reality* (New York: Harper Collins Publishers, 2006), 31.

puts it this way: "What we believe, what we think, and what we do have become so integrated that we are what we are."[112] The highest level of integrity among disciples should be the same whether they are at church, at the supermarket, in their home, or at school.

The characteristic of "humility" is a virtue that millennials desire in church leaders.

The characteristic of "humility" is a virtue that millennials desire in church leaders. Many churches are falling apart as a result of questionable integrity among their leaders. Millennials' understanding of Scripture calls for humility among all Christians, particularly among Christian leaders. Millennials can easily pick up on those with false humility. They are looking for churches where leaders are people of unquestionable integrity. They are not reacting to any particular negative situation as much as they are seeing how Scripture paints a picture of Christian leaders. Millennials just expect Christian leaders to be who the Bible says they are. Peter said, "Therefore humble yourselves under the mighty hand of God, that He may exalt you in due time" (1 Peter 5:6). And the best example of this humility is found in Philippians 2:5-11, where Paul tells

---

[112] David Canada, *Spiritual Leadership in the Small Membership Church* (Nashville: Abingdon Press, 2005), 11.

disciples that they are to have the mind of Christ. They are to do what Christ would do by making themselves of no reputation, in humility and obedience. Leaders need to understand the importance of being good, mature disciples themselves in order to produce mature disciples. Leaders are call to be humble servants. John MacArthur says this about servant leadership: "This is the whole point of servant leadership. We are servants, leading and training other servants; thus, the ministry becomes a self-perpetuating school for servants."[113] Jesus said, "Just as the Son of Man did not come to be served, but to serve, and to give His life a ransom for many" (Matthew 20:28). Kennon L. Callahan notes, "Leaders learn to be leaders. People are not born leaders. Leadership is not a matter of genes or heredity, size or stature. Leaders are not manufactured, the product of some neat and nifty methodology".[114] Leaders are critical because they are God's representatives, and throughout history God has always worked through the principle of representation.

Fifth, there must be sound biblical preaching. Jesus Christ is not only the chief cornerstone of the church, but the Bible, God's Holy Word, is the disciple's foundation. Paul tells Timothy, "All scripture is given by inspiration of God, and is profitable for doctrine, for reproof, for correction, for instruction

---

[113] John MacArthur, *The Book of Leadership* (Nashville: Nelson Books, 2004), 175.
[114] Kennon L. Callahan, *Effective Church Leadership* (New York: Harpers & Row Publishers, 1990), 141.

in righteousness, that the man of God may be complete, thoroughly equipped for ever good work" (2 Timothy 3:16-7). The Bible is God's infallible, inerrant Word, and the foundation for everything a disciple does. The Bible is eternally true and will endure forever. The prophecy of Isaiah says, "The grass withers, the flower fades, But the word of our God stands forever" (Isaiah 40:8). On the day of Pentecost, Peter gave a clear exposition of the gospel; and in this twenty-first century, pastors and ministers must do the same. Tony Evans notes, "Biblical preaching confronts men and women with God through His Word, inspired and energized by the Holy Spirit, filtered through the personality of the pastor, so that the church will understand and respond to Him. Proclamation involves reading, explaining, and applying the Word."[115] It is just not enough to say what the text says. In the old way of preaching, gospel ministers used systematic theology as the basis for their preaching: God, sin, Christ, faith and a little grace. Now the focus must be on the kingdom of God: the creation, the fall, the redemption and restoration provided by the resurrection. There must be user-friendly, transparent gospel presentations of the Word of God. What preaching should ultimately do is persuade those who are lost to accept and embrace Jesus Christ as their personal Savior. Timothy Keller notes, "What Christians think is true and reasonable now appears to be sheer madness to

---

[115] Tony Evans, *God's Glorious Church* (Chicago: Moody Publishers, 2003), 128.

increasing numbers of the population."[116] So how do pastors and ministers preach to skeptical, unfamiliar, and unbelieving people? How can they reach unbelievers influenced heavily by the world? Andy Stanley said, "The question you must answer is, to what extreme are you willing to go to create a delivery system that will connect with the heart of your audience? Are you willing to abandon a style, an approach, a system that was designed in another era for a culture that no longer exists?"[117] Pastors need to communicate for life change. They need to analyze the audience. A congregation is made up of children, teenagers, young adults, seniors, and college students. They all have their own needs and want to hear from the Lord for their particular need. Preachers must analyze the needs of their audience from Sunday to Sunday, or they will miss the mark of the everyday business of the people. They need to know who is out there, what they believe, and what they know or believe about God. They must preach both the holiness of God and the love of God to convey the richness of grace. Keller notes, "Only when people see God as absolutely holy and absolutely loving will the cross of Jesus truly electrify and change them. Jesus was so holy that He had to die for us; nothing less would satisfy his holy and righteous nature. But He

---

[116] Timothy Keller, *Preaching: Communicating Faith in an Age of Skepticism* (New York: Penguin Books, 2015), 94.
[117] Andy Stanley and Lane Jones, *Communicating for a Change* (New York, New York: Multnomah books, 2006), 89.

was so loving that He was glad to die for us; nothing less would satisfy His desire to have us as His people."[118] In addition, Paul encourages those who preach the gospel, "to speak the truth in love." Michael D. Miller states, "Out of a heart that grows in Christlikeness comes a heart for the people to whom you minister. As you hear from God and then speak the truth in love, you demonstrate your heart for God's people."[119]

An effective preaching style for the twenty-first century is narrative preaching.

An effective preaching style for the twenty-first century is narrative preaching. Some people think that expository preaching is boring. Narrative preaching is more storytelling, and it can be both engaging and exciting. Jesus's preaching was exciting because of His stories and images. He captured the ear and heart of the listener. Those who proclaim the gospel should desire the Scriptures to jump off the pages of the Bible and directly into the lives of the people. Congregations respond better to metaphor and imagery, and many young people are used to seeing images all the time: television, iPhone to include Facetime, Facebook, Instagram, and other forms of media.

---

[118] Keller, *Preaching: Communicating Faith in an Age of Skepticism,* 77.
[119] Michael D. Miller, *Keeping Your Heart For Ministry* (Nashville: LifeWay Press, 2001), 35.

Miller notes, "For all listeners hear with words but store what we hear in pictures."[120] The biblical text should control all sermon narratives. Miller further states, "To be all-inclusive is to mix the sermon's content with good stories that illumine the precepts and to teach the precepts that apply the stories to the truth of the text. The best model is not so much a linear trail but a stacked sandwich."[121]

With narrative preaching or any other style, there must be caution against watering down the gospel, giving a shallow theology, or offering a false sense of spirituality. Good biblical exegesis is sometimes the exception rather than the rule. An emphasis on holiness, sacrifice, and commitment is seldom heard. Feel-good and self-esteem sermons are the spiritual food often served to many congregations. Some even give a motivational message that focuses more on God's grace and love, to the neglect of personal accountability. Paul tells Timothy, "Preach the word! Be ready in season *and* out of season. Convince, rebuke, exhort, with all longsuffering and teaching. For the time will come when they will not endure sound doctrine" (2 Timothy 4:2-3). The lack of sound doctrine produces churches that overemphasize legalism on the one hand or emotionalism on the other. The tragedy of all of this is an unstable doctrinal foundation that ultimately will collapse under

---

[120] Calvin Miller, *Preaching: The Art of Narrative Exposition* (Grand Rapids: Baker Books, 2006), 145.
[121] Ibid., 149-150.

pressure. John Blattner wrote, "Sufficient teaching should equip the congregation for deeper relationships with God, family and others in the community. The better they are prepared, the better equipped they will be to minister to others."[122] Tony Evans said, "Many Christians are suffering from spiritual anorexia, starving themselves even though God has provided rich spiritual nourishment in His Word."[123]

Sixth, in this twenty-first century disciples must engage the world through "faithful presence." What this "faithful presence" means is the exercise of a disciple's faith, hope and love toward family, friends, and neighbors, anywhere and everywhere disciples have a sphere of influence (neighborhoods, jobs, schools, governments, cooperate America, etc.). It is engaging the world in a whole new way. James Davison Hunter said, "If there are benevolent consequences of our engagement with the world, in other words, it is precisely because it is not rooted in a desire to change the world for the better but rather because it is an expression of a desire to honor the creator of all goodness, beauty, and truth, a manifestation of our loving obedience to God, and a fulfilment of God's command to love our neighbor."[124] Hunter further notes, "The practice of faithful presence generates relationships and institutions

---

[122] John C. Blattner, *Leading Christians to Maturity* (Alamonte Springs: Creation House, 1987), 39.
[123] Tony Evans, *Life Essentials* (Chicago: Moody Press, 2003), 121.
[124] James Davison Hunter, *To Change the World: The Irony, Tragedy, & Possibility of Christianity in the Late Modern World*, 1st ed. (Oxford: Oxford University, 2010), 235.

that are fundamentally covenantal in character, the ends of which are the fostering of meaning, purpose, truth, beauty, belonging, and fairness—not just for Christians but for everyone."[125] David Fitch adds, "Faithful presence names the reality that God is present in the world and that he uses a people faithful to his presence to make himself concrete and real amid the world's struggles and pain."[126] Jesus modeled this way of living. Jesus was omnipotent, but He always used His power for the good of others. H. Brevy Cannon wrote, "Today's Christians must coherently address modernity's abiding pluralism, learning how to be Christians in a shared world without striving to dominate and control others."[127]

There are many threats to the mission of the church in the twenty-first century. The first is that of tolerance. The Word of God is calling disciples to be holy, but the world is pushing tolerance. Laws are constantly changing that will ultimately impact the community in which the church resides. So if disciples are not careful, they will find themselves tolerating a lot of unacceptable things in the name of Jesus. Many people would love for Christians to act as though all religions are the same, and they are ready to persecute Christians who hold on

---

[125] Ibid., 263.

[126] David E Fitch, *Faithful Presence: Seven Disciplines That Shape the Church for Mission.* (Downer's Grove: InterVarsity Press, 2016), 10.

[127] H. Brevy Cannon, *"Hunter: "End Cultural Wars", take up "Faithful Presence,"* May 10. 2020. Internet available at: https://news.virginia.edu/content/hunter-end-culture-wars-take-faithful-presence

to their distinctiveness. And to make matters worse, there are disciples who are not adequately trained to address the truth of God's word. Some Protestant denominations do not require their pastors to have any formal training. Paul tells young Timothy in Second Timothy 2:15 (KJV), "Be diligent to present yourself approved to God, a worker who does not need to be ashamed, rightly dividing the word of truth." We must properly proclaim the gospel so people will know why Christians appear to be so exclusive. More than other religions, Christianity leads people to love, to be humble, and to serve their enemies? Whose so-called "exclusive" views will lead to peace on this earth? Whose so-called "exclusive" views offer a peace that surpasses all understanding? Whose so-called exclusive views will lead people to unspeakable joy? At the heart of a disciple's exclusiveness is a man named Jesus, who died even for His enemies. Jesus came to show God's inclusive love for all people, even those who do not accept His love.

The second threat to the mission of the church is the lack of willing disciples for the work of the church. Luke said, "After these things the Lord appointed seventy others also, and sent them two by two before His face into every city and place where He Himself was about to go. Then He said to them, 'The harvest truly *is* great, but the laborers *are* few; therefore, pray the Lord of the harvest to send out laborers into His harvest'" (Luke 10:1-2). Harvest and labor were consistent concepts in

Jesus's teachings. In this Scripture, the disciples were instructed to pray for laborers. Without committed laborers, the harvest could not be brought in. The same is true for the church whether planted or revitalized. Without laborers the church would not exist or grow.

The need for workers was urgent because the harvest was ripe and would rot unless persons moved into the fields to bring the grain in quickly. Jesus' whole life revealed a sense of urgency. Not only did he move from town to town proclaiming the good news of the kingdom and calling people to repentance, but he also sent out his disciples periodically to extend the kingdom. He called disciples to help in the task. We know most about his call to the twelve, but he called others as well, to train and commission as workers.[128]

Rick Warren said, "You're not saved by service, but you are saved for service. In God's Kingdom, you have a place, a purpose, a role, and a function to fulfill. This gives your life great significance and value."[129]

The third threat to the mission of the church is tradition. In a tradition-driven church the favorite objection is, "We've always done it this way" or, "We've never done it that way

---

[128] David W. Shenk and David R. Stutzman, "*Creating Communities of the Kingdom : New Testament Models of Church Planting,*" Scottdale: Herald Press, 1988:36. Internet available at: http://search.ebscohost.com/login.aspx?direct=true&AuthType=ip,uid&db=e000xna&AN=28520&site=ehost-live&scope=site
[129] Warren, *The Purpose Driven Life*, 228.

before." The goal of this type of church is to hold firmly to the past. Any change is seen as negative, and maintaining status quo is seen as stability. Rick Warren states, "Older churches tend to be bound by rules, regulations, and rituals, while younger churches tend to be bound together by a sense of purpose and mission. In some churches, tradition can be such a driving force that everything else, even God's will, becomes secondary." [130] It makes it very difficult for a pastor to come in with a well-defined vision from God in a tradition-driven church. In this twenty-first century, tradition can be a hindrance to planting or revitalizing a church. This is what Jesus said to the Pharisees and scribes in Mark 7:9: "All too well you reject the commandment of God, that you may keep your tradition . . . making the word of God of no effect through your tradition which you have handed down. And many such things you do."

I was sitting in the Waffle House for breakfast one morning. As I was talking with the waitress, she said to me that she was told by one of the other waitresses that I was a pastor. So, she asked me where I pastored and I shared that information with her. She continued to share with me and informed me that she had a bitter taste in her mouth about church and did not attend anymore. She was divorced from her husband and was looking for a new church home. Being curious, I asked

---

[130] Rick Warren, *The Purpose Driven Church* (Grand Rapids, Michigan: Zondervan, 2002), 77.

her why. She informed me that she attended a church one Sunday morning and was escorted out because of the tattoos on her neck and arms. The leaders informed her that tattoos were of the devil and she could not be a member because of them. I apologized to her for what she experienced and encouraged her not to give up on God. I told her that there are churches out there that would embrace her and accept her for who she was and that God would guide her to the right place.

Obviously, this church's rules and regulations took precedence over the soul and healing of this dear lady. In essence, this church would have considered this woman's tattoos as a stain on its reputation. But think about what the members of that church missed in the exchange. They missed the opportunity to embrace her with love and care. They missed the opportunity to share in her healing after coming out of a divorce. They missed the missional opportunity to share the love of Jesus with her. They missed the opportunity of this young lady joining their fellowship. This church was not missional or kingdom-focused. This story is a reminder of what Jesus said to the Pharisees and scribes in Matthew 7:13: "Making the word of God of no effect through your tradition which you have handed down. And many such things you do."

Many churches want to be missional to the world, but have no idea how to be missional at home.

Many churches want to be missional to the world, but have no idea how to be missional at home. If a church is going to be missional, it might have to go against the traditional way of "doing" church. Rather than being tradition-focused, or rule-focused, or program-focused, the missional church prides itself on being mission-focused. And if the church is mission-focused it will be people-focused. In a kingdom-oriented worldview, the target of God's redemptive love is the world, not the church. Jesus didn't say "For God so loved the church," but "God so loved the world" (John 3:16). Believers do not go to church; they are the church. This church described earlier needs to move from a membership culture to a missional culture. McNeal notes, "The missional church engages the community beyond its walls because it believes that is why the church exists."[131] A missional church does not measure itself spiritually by how many people attend church on Sunday. Instead, missional individuals in the church think about God and the lost world and arrange their whole lives, every aspect of their lives, around their faith convictions and put their faith into everyday actions. To be missional is a way of life, not an affiliation or activity. To think and to live missionally means seeing all of life as a way to be engaged with the mission of God in the world. For a church to be missional, it must undo Christianity

---

[131] McNeal, 6.

as a religion. There are at least three things the church must do to be missional in the twenty-first century.

First, the church's focus must shift from internal to external. Churches will need to come out of the country club mentality and embrace the community in which they reside. The church needs to be approachable and welcoming to the community. Many churches are so inwardly focused that they don't even realize that cultures are changing in their communities. From the mission statement to the activities in which they are engaged, churches must make their focus more outward. In many of these internally-focused churches, the community is seen only as a source of greater attendance and increased financial gifts. Rainer notes, "Millennial Christians resist this view of the community. For them community is not a place where we look for prospects to help our church; it is a place where Christians are called to serve and minister. Millennials don't ask what the community can do for the church; they ask what they can do for the community."[132] Pastors need to be the leaders in community outreach and evangelism. Robert C. Anderson notes, "The church's ministry must maintain a happy balance where evangelism and edification are in close harmony, to the end that God may be glorified."[133]

---

[132] Rainer and Rainer, 260.

[133] Robert C. Anderson, *The Effective Pastor: A Practical Guide to the Ministry* (Chicago: The Moody Press, 1985), 237.

Second, the program development of the church must be leading members to spiritual maturity. Members should be growing and maturing in the knowledge of Christ. Any special programs (revivals, Sunday school, Bible study groups, youth ministries, college ministries, single ministries, etc.) should be leading disciples to spiritual maturity and growth. Mature leaders, in-turn, will produce more mature leaders. The church must be serious about the spiritual maturity of its members, and not just for knowledge sake. Disciples must put what they are learning into practice. Ted Haggard makes this statement: "Life-giving worship is not just singing, nor is it a three-song warm-up for the sermon. Life-giving worship doesn't only happen when we gather for Sunday services, nor is it an event; it's our lifestyle."[134]

Third, the missional church must move from being church/religious-based to kingdom based. For a church to be kingdom-focused, it must truly understand the importance of the great commission and the great commandments. Believers must love God will all their hearts, souls, and minds, and their neighbors as themselves. The church has been given the commission to go and make disciples, teaching them the commandments of God, and baptizing them in the name of the Father, the Son and the Holy Spirit. The kingdom of God is here now and it is a circumcision of the hearts of men and

---

[134] Ted Haggard, *The Life Giving Church* (Ventura: Regal Books, 1998), 160.

women. Loving God and having a heart for lost people will be the voice of the missional church in a post-secular world. The church in the Waffle House story lost its first love.

In conclusion, the voice of the missional church in the twenty-first century must be one of love and care for others. Disciples must have a burning heart for lost souls, driven by the great commandments and the great commission.

"The great tragedy today is that there are not enough Christians who know who they are."

— **Dr. Zackary Johnson, Sr.**

ACKNOWLEDGMENTS

I want to first acknowledge Bethel Bible Missionary Church where I accepted Jesus Christ as my personal Savior in 1983. Under the leadership of Pastor Vardrey Fleming and his Bible teaching, I was able to grow and mature in the Word of God. I want to also thank Rev. Randy Holloway who was also there at the time, but currently the pastor of Bethel Bible Baptist Church in Greenwood, SC for his inspirational preaching and teaching of the Word.

I want to acknowledge Reedy Fork Baptist Church under the leadership of Pastor T. E. Simmons. I want to thank Pastor Simmons for his leadership and guidance that lead me to accept the call to ministry in 1994. Your leadership gave me the opportunity and confidence to preach and teach the Word of God. In addition, I want to thank the Reedy Fork Church family for embracing my wife and me during our tenure there.

I want to thank the Golden View Baptist Church family for giving me the opportunity to serve as their pastor since 2003. I want to thank you for your love, care and support. Thank you for all of the financial gifts that have also made it possible for me to finance my doctoral expenses. The things that I have learned as your pastor have been rewarding to the pursuit of this degree.

To my professors at Erskine Theological Seminary who have poured into me with their knowledge: Dr. Loyd Melton, Dr. Ralph Gore. Dr. Michael Miller, and Dr. Robert Holmes. A special thanks to my mentor and advisor, Dr. Stephen Clyborne—thank you for challenging me to the best of my ability to produce a quality book. Thank you for all of your time, dedication and energy. We were able to feed off each other through dialogue and collaboration. I want to thank Robin Broome and Jordan Turner for their guidance through registration and finance.

Finally. I want to acknowledge several friends and organizations that have encouraged me along the way: Jimmie and Minister Anna Cecil, Rev. Russell Oglesby, Bishop Gettis Jackson, Dr. Sonia Cunningham-Leverette, Dr. Toney Parks, Dr. Florica Saracut, Dr. James Williams, Dr. Roy Williams, Rev. Sean Dogan, Rev. James Nesbitt, Rev. Curtis Johnson, Dr. Curtis and Louise Hill, Rev. Kenneth and Mercedes Dean, Tommie and Terry Williams, Ron and Lois Thompson, Cleveland

and Angie Beaufort, Rev. W.C. Honeycutt, Rev. Alex Sands, Rev. Rondey Bolden, Jean Hunt, Lennie Beamon, Roberta Davis, Sabrina Sanders, Dr. Wendy Childress, Dorothy Whitner, Jeanette Cherry, Daniel Scott, Rev. Lester Smalls, Rudolph Hall, Earnest Smith, James Starnes, Dr. Phillip Baldwin, Deborah Hamilton, Cathy Stowers, Minister Viola Austin, Fellow Greenville Technical Charter High School Board members to include Principal Mary Nell Anthony; Fellow South Carolina State University Alumni Association Greenville, SC chapter members; SCSU Class of 1974; Brothers of Kappa Alpha Psi, Fraternity. Inc., and the 100 Black Men of the Upstate.

CONTACTING THE AUTHOR

The author can be contacted at
zackaryjohnson@bellsouth.net for book signings,
speaking engagements and bulk purchases.

BIBLIOGRAPHY

Achtemeier, Paul J. *Harper's Bible Dictionary*. San Francisco, California: Harper & Row Publishers, 1985.

Adsit, Christopher B. *Personal Discipleship: A Step-By- Step Guide for Leading a Christian from New Birth to Maturity*. Orlando, Florida: Integrated Resources, 1998.

Anderson, Robert C. *The Effective Pastor: A Practical Guide to the Ministry*. Chicago, Illinois: The Moody Press, 1985.

Blattner, John C. *Leading Christians to Maturity*. Alamonte Springs, Florida: Creation House, 1987.

Bonhoeffer, Dietrich. The Cost of Discipleship. New York, New York: Macmillan Publishing Co., 1979.

Callahan, Kennon L. *Effective Church Leadership*. New York, New York: Harpers & Row Publishers, 1990.

Canada, David. *Spiritual Leadership in the Small Membership Church*. Nashville, Tennessee: Abingdon Press, 2005.

Cannon. H. Brevy, *"Hunter: "End Cultural Wars," take up "Faithful Presence,"* May 10, 2020. Internet available at: https://news.virginia.edu/content/hunter- end culture-wars-take-faithful-presence

Cannon, William R. *The Book of Acts.* Nashville, Tennessee: Upper Room Books, 1989.

Carson, D. A. *Christ and Culture Revisited.* Grand Rapids, Michigan. William B. Eerdmans Publishing, 2008.

Carson, D. A. *Matthew: Expositor's Bible Commentary.* Grand Rapids, Michigan: Zondervan, 1984.

Carter, Joe. *"Why is Church Membership in America on the Decline?"* The Gospel Coalition, March 31, 2021. Internet available at: Why Is Church Membership in America on the Decline? (thegospelcoalition.org)

Chrinian, Eugene. *"Top Characteristics of Generation X Consumers."* May 3, 2016.Internet available at: 7 of the Top Characteristics of Generation X Consumers | Eugene Chrinian (wordpress.com)

Clark, Agatha. *"Millennial Generation Characteristics."* September 29, 2017, Internet available at: Millennial Generation Characteristics (synonym.com)

Cloud, Dr. Henry. *Integrity: the courage to meet the demands of reality.* New York, New York: Harper Collins Publishers, 2006.

Cole, Neil. *Search and Rescue: Becoming A Disciple Who Makes A Difference.* Grand Rapids, Michigan: Baker Books, 2008.

Davies, W. D. and Allison Jr., Dale C. *Matthew 8-18: International Critical Commentary.* New York, New York: Bloomsbury T&T Clark, 1991.

DeHaan, M. R. *Pentecost and After.* Grand Rapids, Michigan: Zondervan Publishing House, 1964.

Dickson, Kwesi A. *The Story of the Early Church.* London, England: Darton, Longman, & Todd Ltd, 1976.

Dodson, Jonathan K. *God-Centered Discipleship.* Wheaton, Illinois: Crossway, 2012.

Donahue, John R. *The Gospel in Parables.* Minneapolis, Minnesota: Fortress Press, 1990.

Eiesland, Nancy and Warner, R. Stephen. *Studying Congregation.* Nashville, Tennessee: Abingdon Press, 1998.

Eims, Leroy. *Disciples in Action.* Colorado Springs, Colorado: Navpress, 1981.

Evans, Tony. *God's Glorious Church.* Chicago, Illinois: Moody Publishers, 2003.

Evans, Tony. *Life Essentials.* Chicago, Illinois: Moody Press, 2003.

Evans, Tony. *Our God is Awesome.* Chicago, Illinois: Moody Press, 1994.

Evans, Tony. *The Promise.* Chicago, Illinois: Moody Press, 1996.

Evans, Tony. *What a Way to Live.* Nashville. Tennessee: Word Publishing, 1997.

Evans, Tony. (n.d.) *"The Process of Discipleship."* Accessed December 15, 2020. Internet available at: https://tonyevans.org/the-process-of-discipleship/

Fitch, David E. *Faithful Presence: Seven Disciplines That Shape the Church for Mission.* Downers Grove, Illinois: InterVarsity Press, 2016.

Gallaty, Robby. *Growing Up: How to Be a Disciple Who Makes Disciples.* Bloomington, IN: Crossbooks, 2013.

GAIA Insights. *"Generation Y Characteristics."* Jan. 2019, Internet available at: Generation Y Characteristics Generation Y

Haggard, Ted. *The Life Giving Church.* Ventura, California: Regal Books, 1998.

Harrington, Bobby and Patrick. *"The Six Elements of a Personal Discipleship Lifestyle."* (Revised 2013). Internet available at: https://cruciform-church.org/wp-content/uploads/2017/03/Discipleship-Handbook.pdf

Henry, Matthew. *Matthew Henry Commentary.* Peabody, Massachusetts: Hendrickson Publishers, Inc., 1991.

Hughes, Richard T. *"Christian America and the Kingdom of God."* University of Illinois Press: 2009. Accessed February 7, 2021. Internet available at: http://ezproxy.erskine.edu:2170/login.aspx?direct=true&AuthType=ip,uid&db=nlebk&AN=569613&site=ehost-live&scope=site

Hull, Bil. *The Complete Book on Discipleship.* Colorado Springs, Colorado: NavPress, 2006.

Hunter, James Davison. *To Change the World: The Irony, Tragedy, & Possibility of Christianity in the Late Modern World*, 1ˢᵗ ed. Oxford, England: Oxford University Press, 2010.

Keller, Timothy. *Center Church.* Grand Rapids, Michigan: Zondervan, 2012.

Keller, Timothy. *Preaching: Communicating Faith in an Age of Skepticism.* New York, New York: Penguin Books, 2015.

Keller, Timothy. *"The Supremacy of Christ in a Postmodern World: Session 3, Desiring God."* 2009. Internet available at: https://www.youtube.com/watch?v=jMLp2mYN_D8

King of Glory AG (n.d.), *"Eight Characteristics of Generation Z."* Internet available at: Eight Characteristics of Generation Z – kingofgloryag.org

Kingsbury, Jack Dean. *Matthew As Story.* Philadelphia, Pennsylvania: Fortress Press, 1988.

Kingsbury, Jack Dean. *Matthew 13: A Study of Redaction Criticism* (Richmond, Virginia: John Knox Press, 1969.

Kirk, Andrew. *The Good News of the Kingdom Coming.* Downers Grove, Illinois: Intervarsity, 1983.

Krodel, Gerhard. *Acts Proclamation Commentaries.* Philadelphia, Pennsylvania: Fortress Press, 1981.

Lacorne, Denis. *"Religion in America: A Political History,"* New York: Columbia University Press, 1988, Internet available at: http://search.ebscohost.com/login.aspx?direct=true&AuthType=ip,uid&db=e000xna&AN=399886&site=ehost-live&scope=site

Ladd, George Eldon. *The Gospel of the Kingdom.* Grand Rapids. Michigan: Eerdsmans Publishing Company, 1959.

Ladd, George Eldon. *The Presence of the Future.* Grand Rapids, Michigan: Eerdmans, 1974.

Lasor, William Sanford. *Old Testament Survey.* Grand Rapids, Michigan: Eerdmans, 1996.

Maier, John P. *The Vision of Matthew: Christ, Church, and Morality in the First Gospel.* New York, New York: Paulist Press, 1978.

MacArthur, John. *The Book of Leadership.* Nashville, Tennessee: Nelson Books, 2004.

McGee, J. Vernon. *Thru the Bible Commentary, volume 4.* Nashville, Tennessee: Thomas Nelson Publishers, 1983.

McNeal, Reggie. *Missional Renaissance: Changing the Scorecard for the Church.* Hoboken, New Jersey: John Riley & Sons, 2009.

McNeile, Alan Hugh. *The Gospel according to Matthew.* Grand Rapids, Michigan: Baker, 1980.

McSwain, Steve. *"21ˢᵗ Century Church: New Absolutes the Church must Embrace or Die."* The Huffington Post, Dec. 6, 2017. Internet available at: 21st Century Church: New Absolutes the Church Must Embrace or Die (Part 1) | HuffPost

Miller, Calvin. *Preaching: The Art of Narrative Exposition.* Grand Rapids: Baker Books, 2006.

Miller, Michael D. *Keeping Your Heart For Ministry.* Nashville, Tennessee: LifeWay Press, 2001.

Murrell, Steve. *WikiChurch: Making Discipleship Engaging, Empowering, and Viral.* Lake Mary, FL: Charisma House, 2011.

Munroe, Myles. *Rediscovering The Kingdom.* Shippensburg, Pennsylvania: Destiny Image Publishers, 2004.

Niebuhr, H. Richard. *Christ and Culture.* New York, New York: Harper, 1951.

Ogden, Greg. *Transforming Discipleship: Making Disciples a Few at a Time.* Downers Grove: IVP, 2003. *Oxford Advanced Learners Dictionary*, Oxford University Press, 2021, Internet available at: integrity noun - Definition, pictures, pronunciation and usage notes | Oxford Advanced Learner's Dictionary at OxfordLearnersDictionaries.com

Pentecost, J. Dwight. *Thy Kingdom Come.* Wheaton, Illinois: Victor, 1990.

Powell, Mark Allan. *What is Narrative Criticism,* Minneapolis, Minnesota: Fortress Press, 1990.

Putman, Jim. *Real-Life Discipleship: Building Churches That Make Disciples.* Colorado Springs: NavPress, 2010.

Rainer, Thom S. and Eric Geiger. *Simple Church: Returning to God's Process for Making Disciples.* Nashville, Tennessee: Broadman & Holman, 2006.

Rainer, Thom S. *Church Growth and Evangelism in the Book of Acts,* Criswell Theological Review 5.1 (1990). Internet available at: <u>Church Growth and Evangelism in the Book of Acts (gordon.edu)</u>

Riner, Thom S. and Rainer, Jess W. *The Millennials.* Nashville, Tennessee: Broadman and Holman, 2011.

Ramsdell, Thomas J. *"The Kingdom of Heaven in the Gospel."* The Biblical World Vol. 4, No. 2. Chicago: The University of Chicago Press, (August, 1894): 124, Internet available at: <u>https://www.jstor.org/stable/3135427?seq=1#metadata_info_tab_contents</u>

Shenk, David W. and Stutzman, David R. *"Creating Communities of the Kingdom: New Testament Models of Church Planting."* Scottdale: Herald Press, 1988:36, Internet available at: <u>http://search.ebscohost.com/login.aspx?direct=true&AuthType=ip,uid&db=e000xna&AN=28520&site=ehost-live&scope=site</u>

Stanley, Andy and Jones, Lane. *Communicating for a Change.* New York, New York: Multnomah Books, 2006.

Stott, John R. W. *The Message of Acts: The Bible Speaks Today.* Downers Grove, Illinois: InterVarsity Press, 1990.

Twenge, Jean. *Generation Me, Revised/Updated edition*. New York, New York: Atria Books, 2014.

Vine, W. *"World - Vine's Expository Dictionary of New Testament Words."* Blue Letter Bible. 24 Jun, 1996. Web. 31 Jan, 2021. Internet available at: <u>https://www.blueletterbible.org/search/dictionary/viewtopic.cfm</u>

Vines, W. E., M. A. *Entry for 'Humble'.* Vine's Expository Dictionary of NT Words. https://www.studylight.org/dictionaries/eng/ved/h/humble.html. 1940.

Warren, Rick. *The Purpose-Driven Church.* Grand Rapids, Michigan: Zondevan, 1995.

Warren, Rick. *The Purpose Driven Life.* Grand Rapids, Michigan: Zondervan, 2002.

Wenham, David. *The Parables of Jesus.* Downers Grove, Illinois: InterVarsity Press, 1989.

White, James Emery. *Meet Generation Z.* Grand Rapids, Michigan: Baker, 2017.

Wiersbe, Warren W. *Meet Yourself in the Parables.* Wheaton, Illinois: Victor Books, 1979.

Wiersbe, Warren W. *The Integrity Crisis.* Nashville, Tennessee: Thomas Nelson Publishers, 1988.

Whitney, Donald S. *Spiritual Disciplines for the Christian Life.* Colorado Springs, Colorado: Navpress, 1991.

Young, Edward J. *Introduction to the Old Testament.* Grand Rapids, Michigan: Eerdmans, 1960.

Made in the USA
Columbia, SC
14 December 2023

27847376R00111